BFI FILM CLASSICS

. . . .

Rob White
SERIES EDITOR

Edward Buscombe, Colin MacCabe and David Meeker
SERIES CONSULTANTS

Cinema is a fragile medium. Many of the great films now exist, if at all, in damaged or incomplete prints. Concerned about the deterioration in the physical state of our film heritage, the National Film and Television Archive, part of the British Film Institute's Collections Department, has compiled a list of 360 key works in the history of the cinema. The long-term goal of the Archive is to build a collection of perfect showprints of these films, which will then be screened regularly at the National Film Theatre in London in a year-round repertory.

BFI Film Classics is a series of books intended to introduce, interpret and honour these 360 films. Critics, scholars, novelists and those distinguished in the arts have been invited to write on a film of their choice, drawn from the Archive's list. The numerous illustrations have been made specially from the Archive's own prints.

With new titles published each year, the BFI Film Classics series is a unique, authoritative and highly readable guide to the masterpieces of world cinema.

The best movie publishing idea of the [past] decade.
Philip French, *The Observer*

A remarkable series which does all kinds of varied and divergent things.
Michael Wood, *Sight and Sound*

Exquisitely dimensioned . . . magnificently concentrated examples of freeform critical poetry.
Uncut

John Wayne, John Ford and C.V. Whitney filming *The Searchers* (by courtesy of Louise DeWald, Scottsdale, AZ)

BFI FILM CLASSICS

THE SEARCHERS

. . . .

Edward Buscombe

 Publishing

First published in 2000 by the
BRITISH FILM INSTITUTE
21 Stephen Street, London W1P 2LN

The British Film Institute
promotes greater understanding
and appreciation of, and
access to, film and moving image
culture in the UK.

British Library Cataloguing-in-Publication Data
A catalogue record for this book is available from the British Library

ISBN 0–85170–820–X

Series design by
Andrew Barron & Collis Clements Associates

Typeset in Fournier and Franklin Gothic by
D R Bungay Associates, Burghfield, Berks

Printed in Great Britain by The Cromwell Press, Trowbridge, Wiltshire

CONTENTS

ACKNOWLEDGMENTS

All quotations from production memos and letters to Ford are courtesy the Lilly Library, Indiana University, Bloomington, Indiana. Copies of the script of *The Searchers* are lodged in the Lilly Library and in the library of the British Film Institute.

My special thanks for help of various kinds to Corey Creekmur, Ned Comstock, Jim D'Arc, Dan Ford, Tise Vahimagi, Noel King, Art Eckstein, Sandra Archer, Dudley Andrew, Gerald Sim, James Nottage, Mike Thomas, Rob White, Markku Salmi.

For Sarah: 'sure as the turning of the earth'

1
. . . .

A door opens. The camera tracks forward, following a woman outside where, silhouetted against the landscape, she watches a rider approaching. A man comes to stand alongside her and speaks the first word of *The Searchers*. It's a question.

'Ethan?'

The rider dismounts. He is dusty, travel-stained. He wears blue cavalry trousers with a yellow stripe, a grey military coat with a sergeant's chevron, and a black hat blowing in the wind.[1] He holds a sword in its scabbard.

'That's your uncle Ethan,' says his niece Lucy to her brother Ben. Ethan silently shakes his brother Aaron by the hand, then kisses his sister-in-law Martha reverently on the brow. She precedes him into the house, in a strange motion, facing him and walking backwards, almost as if one might walk before royalty.[2] Inside, Ethan sweeps the youngest child, Debbie, up in his arms, holding her high above his head in a gesture he will repeat at the end of the film. Martha takes Ethan's coat. He watches her as she goes into the bedroom and carefully folds it. Aaron watches Ethan; he knows what's going on, but he defuses the potential discord by offering Ethan his hand. 'Thanks, Aaron,' says Ethan, shaking it. Later, after supper, Ethan sits outside alone, with only Chris, the family dog, for company. He looks back inside the house and sees Aaron closing the bedroom door, shutting him out. A great sadness falls over Ethan's face.[3]

The next day there is another scene with Martha and the coat. It's shot in the customary Ford manner: put the camera in just the right place, then have the actors move around it. We're in the main room of the house, with the front door to our left. The Reverend Clayton comes towards the front of the frame and stands there drinking coffee. He glances sideways to his left, screen right. There's a cut, necessary to establish that it's a point-of-view shot, to the back bedroom, in which we see what he sees, Martha holding the coat as if it were a religious relic, stroking it. Cut back to Clayton, who, having inadvertently witnessed this private moment, stares straight ahead. Martha's secret will be safe with him. Behind his back Ethan walks in. Martha comes from the bedroom into the frame from the right, and hands Ethan first his hat, then the coat. He bends and kisses her on the brow, as before. She holds his arm and looks up at him. Clayton continues to stare forward, deliberately not watching what is happening behind him. Ethan walks across the room and out of the door. Martha follows, then stops at the door looking out. Clayton puts down his cup, puts on his hat and squeezes politely through the door past Martha without a word. In the next shot, outside, Ethan and the posse are leaving. Martha comes into the frame with Debbie, watching Ethan leave as she had watched him arrive. Ethan rides away without looking back. It is the last time Martha will see him, though not the last time he will see her.

The secret of Ethan and Martha; Clayton pretends not to notice

There are many questions about Ethan. There's a mystery about his past; where has he been the last few years? He's evasive when questioned by Aaron.

'How was California?'

'California? How should I know?'

Aaron's young son Ben pursues the investigation. As his grey coat suggests, Ethan has been a Confederate soldier. But the Civil War has been over three years, and Ben demands, 'Why didn't you come home before now?' We never do get a precise account of Ethan's movements prior to his arrival. He has a large store of gold coins. Aaron remarks that they are 'fresh-minted' (the implication is they may be stolen from a bank). 'So?' Ethan retorts.

There were a lot of people roaming the West at the end of the Civil War who didn't welcome questions about their movements. Jesse James was another who didn't surrender, didn't turn his sabre 'into no ploughshare, neither', preferring to drift around Missouri robbing banks and trains. The Western is full of discontented Southerners: Benjamin Tyreen in *Major Dundee*, Stonewall Torrey in *Shane*, Ben Allison in *The Tall Men*, Josey Wales in *The Outlaw Josey Wales*, all with a chip on their shoulder, unfinished business to take care of. Like them, Ethan has resisted integration back into society. He's recalcitrant, maybe a renegade; surly and suspicious, he seems to have something to hide.[4]

But about one thing there is no mystery. Ethan is in love with his brother's wife, and she with him. The relationship is delicately sketched in but unmistakable.[5] All Ethan's actions are in the shadow of his illicit desire. It violates the sanctity of his brother's home, and so cannot be expressed. Instead, it turns inwards, there to fester, sending him half-mad with longing and grief.

II

By the time he came to *The Searchers*, John Ford had been in pictures over forty years. Starting as an occasional actor and assistant to his brother Francis, he directed his first feature, *The Tornado*, in 1917. It was a Western. *The Searchers* was his one hundred and fifteenth feature film, and by then he'd become the most respected director in Hollywood, four times winner of the Oscar for Best Director (*The Informer*, *The Grapes of*

Wrath, How Green Was My Valley, The Quiet Man). Yet the middle 50s were not an unmixed triumph for Ford. Some of his projects were uninspired remakes such as *What Price Glory?* and *Mogambo*. Eccentrically personal works like *The Sun Shines Bright* performed poorly at the box office. His drinking was getting worse and there were violent rages, one of which resulted in a fistfight on the set of *Mister Roberts* with its star, Henry Fonda, in 1955. That same year Ford had been reduced to working in television.

But with the right material he was as good as ever; better, in fact. Back in his beloved Monument Valley, with his old friend Merian C. Cooper producing, and his stock company of actors around him whom he could bully to his heart's content and know he'd be forgiven (he and Fonda were never friends again), all the genius came flooding back. Ford began when cinema was silent and he'd learned to tell a story through pictures, learned what to do with a camera (and what not to do). Not that Ford didn't like talk; his writer on *The Searchers*, Frank Nugent, said he had 'a wonderful ear for dialogue'.[6] But where Ford excels is in the way he animates the screen, invests it with vitality and interest. The actors don't just stand there spouting words.

Take the scene at the Edwards' ranch the morning after Ethan's arrival. There's a quick shot outside of the Rangers riding up to the ranch house; smoke blows briskly from the chimney. A wide shot of the interior shows Martha at the back, attending to the oven by the fire. Lucy is serving out what looks like oatmeal; Debbie sits at the table, screen left, Ben on the other side. The dog is barking. There's a knock at the door, Ben gets up, Lucy starts fussing with her dress, mindful of who might be arriving. The camera pans and tracks to the window as Ben, Martha and Lucy crane to see outside, while Aaron crosses into the frame towards the door. Cut to a reframed shot of the door as it opens and a company of Rangers pour through, riding after cattle thieves: Clayton, Jorgensen, Nesby, Charlie McCorry, Mose Harper. Clayton explains their business as Ben, Debbie, Martha, Aaron and Jorgensen group round him.

It's the next shot that shows Ford's true gift for making things come alive, an effect achieved not by busy camera movement or rapid cutting, but by what's actually happening in the frame, the illusion of real life going on before our eyes. The camera is placed more or less where it was when Ethan first entered the house, but this time it stays still for a long time. Clayton sits down at the head of the table, facing the camera. Ben and Debbie resume their seats and Clayton asks Debbie if she's been baptised yet, but he doesn't listen to the answer, ordering Aaron to get Martin. In the background all is bustle, Lucy getting cups from the dresser, Martha bringing the coffee pot from the stove, Mose making a little bow to Martha before seating himself in the rocking chair, Aaron at the back of the frame talking to Charlie and Nesby. Lucy hands a cup to Jorgensen, seated on the left of the frame, and picks up the coffee pot, only for Clayton, who hasn't stopped talking from the start of the shot, to haul her back: 'Wait a minute sister, I didn't get any coffee yet.' At this moment Martin appears at the back of the room, pulling on his jacket, as Martha hands Clayton doughnuts. Lucy rushes towards the back, Martin grabs her hand playfully, but she brushes past him, on her way out back to see her boyfriend Brad, as we discover in the next scene. Clayton starts swearing in Aaron and Martin as Rangers: 'Raise your right hand'; Mose has his left hand stretched out to the fire. 'You will faithfully discharge ...' says Clayton. At this moment the door at the back of the room opens to reveal Ethan, just as Martha moves across it; it's as though she is somehow pulling back a curtain, summoning up his presence. Ben interrupts Clayton, asking to go along. The comically irascible Clayton admonishes him and loses his train of thought. Debbie prompts him: 'faithfully fulfil ...' Clayton ploughs on: 'faithfully discharge ...' Ethan has been slowly walking forward from the back, observed by all except Clayton. Jorgensen rises to ask Martha for coffee. 'Shut up,' shouts Clayton, exasperated at another interruption. As Ethan strolls ever closer, the camera now tracking forward, Clayton eventually completes the swearing in. Aaron calls him Reverend, and Clayton puts him right: 'Just call me Captain.' Ethan has now reached the table and leans forward

Fordian *mise en scène*:
Clayton gets his coffee

on it, to Clayton's astonishment, and addresses him by his full title: 'Captain the Reverend Samuel Johnson Clayton.'[7]

With deft economy, solidity and spontaneity Ford evokes the warm companionship of human life in this little outpost in the wilderness – life that for some will soon be brutally cut short. At the same time, we feel Ethan's intrusiveness; his very presence is a disruption. Clayton, like Ben and Aaron before him, interrogates Ethan. When he offers to swear Ethan into the posse, Ethan replies, 'No need to. Wouldn't be legal anyway.'

'Why not?' Clayton demands. 'You wanted for a crime, Ethan?'

Ethan avoids answering by a further question: 'You got a warrant?'

By the end of the picture Clayton will have one, though it's never served.

III

. . . .

Strictly speaking, 'Ethan?' is not the first word uttered in *The Searchers*, nor the first question. Over the credits we hear the opening stanza and chorus of a song written by Stan Jones and sung by The Sons of the Pioneers, a singing group Ford had earlier used on-screen in *Rio Grande:*

> What makes a man to wander
> What makes a man to roam?
> What makes a man leave bed and board
> And turn his back on home?

> Ride away, ride away, ride away.[8]

Jones had been a ranger in the National Parks Service and first came to Ford's notice while the director was shooting *3 Godfathers* in Death Valley in 1948. Jones had a big hit with 'Ghost Riders in the Sky', and Ford hired him to write songs for *Rio Grande* and *Wagon Master*. Five years on, by the time of *The Searchers*, Elvis Presley had made his first recording and popular music was changed for ever. But Ford didn't mind if the close harmony ballads of The Sons of the Pioneers now sounded dated; his taste in music always ran to the folksy.

The question – What makes a man to wander? – may be specific to Ethan. If so, the opening scenes provide an answer: there is no place for him at home. But perhaps the question is more generally addressed, to us all. Westerns are rarely about settled domestic life, so often about men on their own, on the move. They offer a fantasy of freedom, a dream of a life untrammelled by ties of home or work or the other fences which society surrounds us with. In the wide open spaces of the West a man may ride where he has a mind to. Realistically, in the nineteenth-century world where the Western is set, only men have the economic and physical capacity to pursue such freedom. Jane Tompkins has seen the rise of the Western in fiction in the late nineteenth century as a male flight from the feminisation of culture, escaping to a space from which women are excluded, a counter-balance to 'women's invasion of the public sphere between 1880 and 1920'.[9] But might not women also want, in a part of themselves, to break free from domesticity and its responsibilities, from what Ford in *Stagecoach* ironically calls 'the blessings of civilisation'; might they too not want like Huck Finn to 'light out for the territory'? Don't we all have dreams of leaving?

IV

As we hear the song, the credits of the film play out, in the familiar Playbill typeface favoured by Ford for most of his sound Westerns, set against the backdrop of an adobe wall. Adobe bricks are made of clay mixed with straw or grass, and were used by Pueblo Indians as well as by the Spanish in the Southwest. But this wall provides more than local colour, a signifier of exactly where we are in the West. It evokes the historical context within which the film is set, the violent struggle for supremacy over southern Texas in the mid-nineteenth century. Adobe Walls was the name of a trading post in southwest Texas, and the first Battle of Adobe Walls was fought in 1864 by a force of whites led by Kit Carson against several hundred Comanche. Ten years later came the second Battle of Adobe Walls, in which twenty-eight buffalo hunters held off a large band of Comanche, Cheyenne and Kiowa. From the eighteenth century, when they first arrived on the southern Plains from the north, the Comanche had been involved in a series of wars against the Spanish, then the Mexicans, then the Texans. (Texas had become independent of Mexico in 1836, then joined the Union in 1845.) The Texas Rangers, in which the Reverend Clayton is a Captain, were an irregular force, formed in 1835, mainly to fight the Indians. Warfare between the Texas settlers and the Comanche was endemic for a generation, culminating in the Red River War of 1874–5 which finally destroyed the Comanche's military strength.[10]

V

In the opening shot of the film, the view from the Edwards' ranch is of a landscape partly obscured by dust. When the band of Rangers ride out next day we get our first good look at Monument Valley. The clarity of the air is astonishing. Buttes that must be twenty miles away rise sharply in focus; the sense of space and distance takes one's breath away. *The Searchers* was Ford's fifth film in this location, beginning with *Stagecoach* seventeen years previously.[11] Elsewhere I've described how, in the course of the nineteenth century, American tastes in landscape were transformed, from a European-derived preference for mountains, lakes and trees, to an appreciation of the distinctively American topography of the Southwest, its deserts, canyons and mesas.[12] In *The Southwest in American Literature and Art*, David W. Teague traces the rise of what he calls 'a desert aesthetic': 'by 1910 deserts had become associated with the very height of American culture. They were developing into the aesthetic wonderlands that gave rise to the nature writing of Mary Austin, the art of Georgia O'Keeffe, the photographs of Alfred Stieglitz …'[13] Nationalism played its part in this transformation, that same desire to extol American exceptionalism which we find in Frederick Jackson Turner's 'frontier thesis', first developed at the end of the nineteenth century to show how the experience of the Western frontier decisively shaped the American character and made it different from the European.[14] The artist Maynard Dixon, who devoted himself to capturing the spirit of the arid Southwest during the 20s and 30s, wrote:

[W]hat art is vital that does not grow out of the psychic and material life of the country that produces it? It is not only possible but necessary for us artists to look more frankly at the conditions and country surrounding us, to go directly to them as a source of inspiration and to work out our own interpretation of them. … If we are to have anything that can be called a vital American art it must come this way; not by the obedient repetition of European formulas, but through the ability and courage of our artists to take the life and the material of their own country and out of these express their aspiration.[15]

It was science which had first given these new kinds of landscape their significance, specifically the science of geology. As Stephen Pyne shows in *How the Canyon Became Grand*, the Grand Canyon became a kind of Aladdin's Cave for American geologists in the last quarter of the nineteenth century. The 5,000-feet deep chasm revealed nothing less than the history of the earth over successive aeons. In Pyne's words, 'The Canyon became to geology what the Louvre was to art or St Peter's Square to architecture',[16] playing a key role in the transformation not only of the aesthetics of landscape but of conceptions of history and of life itself. As the result of geological discoveries, Pyne says

> Between the late eighteenth century and the mid-twentieth, the known age of the earth increased a millionfold, from less than 6,000 years to more than 4.6 billion. The determination of the exact scale of geologic time and how to organize its unfathomable domain remained the particular province of geology. Upon its conclusions rested the mechanics of organic evolution, and upon those mechanics depended the program of social progress. The age of the earth decided whether Darwinian evolution by natural selection, with its immense drafts of time, was possible. The debate over models of organic evolution informed discussions over moral progress and the future of civilizations.[17]

When we look at the eroded landscapes of the Southwest it is impossible not to be in awe of their great age, the almost unimaginable stretches of time needed to hew the canyons from the rock, or to grind and wash away the valley floor, leaving the huge mesas standing clear. There are two kinds of time in *The Searchers*, that of the long and lonely years which elapse as Marty and Ethan pursue their quest, and the immensely longer geological time which puts all human acts into another perspective, which renders them puny in comparison, but more poignant.

Pyne also charts how the kind of landscape art which valorised the beauties of the Canyon became itself fossilised by the rise of Modernism.[18] Led by Thomas Moran, whose efforts were financially supported by the Santa Fe railroad in order to encourage tourism in the Southwest, artists descended on such picturesque spots in ever increasing numbers during the first quarter of the twentieth century, to produce paintings which, remaining dedicated to nineteenth-century ideas of fidelity to nature, were innocent of the new ideas in art. The movies, never greatly interested in Modernism anyway, were eager to cash in on the popular visual appeal of the canyons, deserts and mesas. Deserts also played an important part in the novels of Zane Grey, by far the most popular author of Westerns in the first third of the twentieth century, and the writer most influential in shifting the popular imagination towards the Southwest. On his first trip west in 1907, he had visited the Grand Canyon on horseback and immediately fell under the spell of south-western scenery, using it as the setting of the first of his many bestsellers, *The Heritage of the Desert*, published in 1910. Over the course of the next twenty years Grey produced a stream of novels with southwestern settings, such as *Desert Gold, Wanderer of the Wasteland, Call of the Canyon* and *Under the Tonto Rim. Wildfire*, published in 1917, is set in Monument Valley itself. Grey's work had a powerful influence upon Hollywood's use of landscape in the late 10s and 20s, and his novels were seized upon by film-makers anxious to exploit his huge popularity. In 1918 came films of *Riders of the Purple Sage, The Light of Western Stars* and *The Rainbow Trail*. Five more Zane Grey films followed the next year, with Grey insisting on authentic southwestern locations.

The desert aesthetic was tailor-made for Hollywood. By 1910 Westerns were the most popular film genre, Los Angeles had become firmly established as a film-making centre, and desert scenery was right on the doorstep. William S. Hart frequently favoured desert settings for his films, as in *The Scourge of the Desert* (1915) and *The Desert Man* (1917). All the top Western stars of the 20s followed suit: Tom Mix in *Desert Love* (1920), Jack Hoxie in *A Desert Bridegroom* (1922), Harry Carey in *Desert Driven* (1923), Buck Jones in *The Desert Outlaw* (1924), Tom Tyler in *The Desert Pirate* (1927) and Tim McCoy in *The Desert Rider* (1929).

Ford's first colour film shot in Monument Valley was *She Wore a Yellow Ribbon* in 1949. Winton Hoch, the cameraman, won an Oscar for it. Hoch had joined Technicolor on graduating from Cal Tech and, it's claimed, never shot a foot of monochrome film.[19] He'd started with Ford on *3 Godfathers* in 1948, and before *The Searchers* had also done *The Quiet*

Man and *Mister Roberts*. No Ford picture, indeed no American picture, makes such sumptuous use of landscape as *The Searchers*. Hollywood narrative film doesn't let us dwell long on the beauties of scenery; the story must move forward. But there are many times in *The Searchers* when one is begging Ford to indulge us just a little more, to let our eyes feast on the stately towers of red sandstone standing mighty against the azure sky, or roam the vastness of the space that dwarfs the tiny riders.

One reason that the landscape has such grandeur, besides the sureness of Ford's eye for composition and Hoch's undoubted skill, is that the movie was filmed in VistaVision. When CinemaScope was introduced by 20th Century-Fox in 1953, Paramount had refused to use the new system, preferring a widescreen process of its own. Instead of the anamorphic camera lens which CinemaScope used to compress the wide image onto standard 35mm film (the picture was then expanded back by another lens during projection), VistaVision switched the negative film through ninety degrees and exposed it horizontally, as in a 35mm still camera. This effectively doubled the area of the frame, giving extremely sharp pictures in a ratio of 1.85:1 (compared to the 1.33:1 standard or 'Academy' ratio, and the 2.35:1 of CinemaScope). The other great advantage was that VistaVision prints could be made from the large negative onto standard 35mm film, which did not require theatres to install any new equipment.

VI

. . . .

The little band of Rangers are riding in pursuit of some cattle that have been driven off from the nearby ranch of Lars Jorgensen, played by John Qualen, who, of Norwegian origin himself, played a series of gently comic Scandinavians in other Ford Westerns (Ole Knudsen in *Two Rode Together*, Peter Ericson in *The Man Who Shot Liberty Valance*, Svenson in *Cheyenne Autumn*). He and the Reverend Clayton are accompanied by old Mose (Hank Worden), by another rancher, Nesby (William Steele), by Charlie McCorry, played by Ken Curtis, and by Jorgensen's son Brad, who is romancing Ethan's niece Lucy and is played by Harry Carey Jr, son of the silent Western star Harry Carey (of whom more anon).[20] Ford was famous for keeping a tightly knit group around him. Four of the actors, John Wayne, Ward Bond, Harry Carey Jr and Hank Worden, had between them made a total of sixteen previous appearances in Ford Westerns, besides many of his other films. Other Ford veterans in *The Searchers* include Harry Carey's wife Olive, who as Mrs Jorgensen is mother in the film to her real-life son Harry Jr, and in minor roles, Jack Pennick and stuntman and bit player Chuck Roberson. Colonel Greenhill is played by Cliff Lyons, who was, as usual, in charge of the stunt crew, most of whom were also veterans of Ford pictures.

It's a film about family, as Ford's films often are. We're on the edge of the frontier. There's no community to speak of, no civil society; just small family groups, as at the dawn of the human race. There's Ethan and his brother Aaron, Aaron's wife Martha and their three children, Lucy, Debbie and Ben. They have adopted Marty, whose parents have been killed. Their neighbours are the Jorgensens, mother, father, son Brad and daughter Laurie. The Comanche chief, Scar, has a family too; we see four wives in his tepee and hear of two sons, both killed by whites. Even the army is a family affair: Colonel Greenhill commands his son, Lieutenant Greenhill.

And it's a film which contains families. Besides the Careys, there are the Wood sisters, Natalie and Lana, both playing Debbie. John Wayne's son Pat plays Lieutenant Greenhill. Producer Merian Cooper cast his wife, Dorothy Jordan, as Martha, and Ford cast his son-in-law Ken Curtis (married to his daughter Barbara) as Charlie. Ford's son Pat was associate producer, and the brother of Ford's wife, Wingate Smith, was assistant director. Was there ever so much benevolent nepotism in a single film?

Ethan has offered to join the Rangers in the search for the cattle. His motive is presumably self-sacrificing, leaving Aaron at home with Martha in the safety of the homestead. It is a fatal misjudgement. He's accompanied by Martin Pawley (Jeffrey Hunter) who, like Ethan, has been introduced riding towards an open door, but coming in at a clip, accompanied by some jaunty music and leaping off his horse. Martin, we learn, is one-eighth Cherokee. From the beginning Ethan will treat him with barely disguised hostility, cruelly rejecting the young man's friendly overtures solely, it appears, because of his racial origin (emphasised by brown make-up). 'A man could mistake you for a half-breed,' Ethan growls at him. Ethan is a racist *before* the murder of Martha.

On the trail of the missing cattle the Rangers soon discover evidence that they have been driven off not by rustlers but by Indians, in order to divert them away from the now unprotected ranches. And not just any Indians, but the most feared ('ain't Caddos, ain't Kiowas, Comanch [sic] sure', says Mose). As Ethan contemplates the fate of Martha and the others, the camera dwells on his face, gazing bleakly into the distance as he wipes the sweat from his horse, and we foresee the tragedy that is to come.

VII

Reining in at the top of a ridge overlooking the homestead the next day, Ethan sees it's on fire. Striding through the smoke and flames, crying 'Martha, Martha', he finds a blue dress. It is the one Martha wore. He looks into the store-house. The camera is inside, framing him against the light. We cannot see his face, but he bends his head in grief; evidently it is Martha's body he has seen. He tells Mose not to let Marty see inside: 'Won't do him any good.' Mose draws what comfort he can from righting the rocking chair and sits minding Marty, while the dog draws Ethan's attention to Debbie's discarded doll.

Martha, we infer, has been raped and murdered by the Comanche. Aaron and Ben are dead too, though this hardly seems to register with Ethan. Lucy and Debbie have been captured. Now the shape of the story is clear. It's a captivity narrative; but also a revenge plot.

An authentically American story-structure, the captivity narrative may be traced back at least as far as the seventeenth century, when Mary Rowlandson was captured by Indians during King Philip's War in 1676. Eventually taken back into white society, she published her story in 1682. It went through four editions in the first year alone. Over the next two centuries, to be captured by Indians was a not uncommon experience; thousands of whites, mainly women and children, underwent this fate. Many were taken for ransom, others were adopted into Indian tribes. Their experiences were frequently documented, and in the nineteenth century alone several hundred such accounts were published. Few types of narrative exert as visceral a hold on the reader, who experiences a terrifying yet pleasurable thrill in the story of one, less fortunate than themselves, who falls into the hands of the enemy. Such a basic narrative structure can be adapted to any genre, even children's stories. In a particularly spine-chilling example, *The Tale of Samuel Whiskers, or The*

Roly-Poly Pudding by Beatrix Potter, Tom Kitten is captured by the rats who live behind the skirting board and is rolled up in pastry to be made into a pudding. Stories of humans kidnapped by aliens are a more contemporary version.

Already successful as biography, the captivity narrative became a mainstay of Western fiction in the novels of James Fenimore Cooper. Not surprisingly, the Western movie has exploited its potential in such films as *Northwest Passage, Unconquered, Comanche Station, Soldier Blue, A Man Called Horse, Little Big Man* and *Dances with Wolves,* besides Ford's own *Two Rode Together.*

Though violation of female captives by Indians was apparently the exception, it did occur, and in the nineteenth century some narratives pruriently focused on the sexual outrages suffered by white women. The title page of *History of the Captivity and Providential Release of Mrs. Caroline Harris,* published in 1838, records how Mrs Harris and her female friend were forced to become 'the companions of, and to cohabit with, two disgusting Indian Chiefs ... from whom they received the most cruel and beastly treatment'.[21] Yet contrary to the opportunity such stories gave of demonising the Indians, in many accounts the captives 'went native', some electing to stay with their captors even when offered release, a decision profoundly troubling to a white society convinced of its superiority.[22] One analysis suggests that 'the prime candidate for transculturation was a girl aged seven through fifteen'.[23] Ethan's fear is thus two-fold: that the two captured girls will be raped, the 'fate worse than death' of Victorian melodrama, and/or that they will be absorbed into Indian society, losing their white identity. In the event, both fears are realised. Ethan soon discovers that Lucy has suffered an identical fate to Martha's. And when finally he catches up with Debbie, she is the wife of a Comanche and has all but become Comanche herself, referring to them as 'my people'.

The shape and direction of the film are now clear. It will be the story of Ethan's mission, to avenge the rape and murder of Martha, and to rescue Debbie. But as time passes Ethan realises that Debbie will be changed by her experience. In the event, we learn almost nothing of her life in captivity. All we know is what is festering in Ethan's mind; what obsesses him is not the general process of transculturation she must be undergoing, it's the thought of her having sex with Indians that eats away at him. He can hardly bring himself to articulate it. As he says to Marty before their first return to the Jorgensens', after a year, 'they'll keep her to raise as one of their own until … until she's of an age to …' He cannot finish the sentence. By the time they find her she's reached puberty. Ethan's response is to try to kill her. 'She's been living with a buck,' he says to Marty in justification. 'She's nothing but a …'; he cannot find the word. Miscegenation is unbearable to him; it must be effaced by murder.

But it's more than just the horror of an Indian having sex with a white woman that drives Ethan. You don't have to be a psychoanalyst to intuit that Scar, the Comanche chief whom Ethan implacably pursues, is in some sense Ethan's unconscious, his id if you like. In raping Martha, Scar has acted out in brutal fashion the illicit sexual desire which Ethan harboured in his heart. Ethan's assumption of the role of justified avenger, wreaking upon Scar the punishment he deserves, allows him to assume the high moral ground. But his self-righteousness, as in the killing of Futterman, an act which raises some eyebrows, can be seen as an attempt to blot out his own guilt.

When at the end of the film Ethan finally catches up with Scar he finds him already dead, shot by Marty. Drawing his knife, he scalps Scar in a symbolic act of castration. Once Scar's sexual threat has been neutered, Ethan's desire for revenge is assuaged and instead of killing Debbie, his expressed intention, he takes her home. But for Ethan his transgressive desire for his brother's wife means there is no place in the home, no family he can be integrated into. Ride away.

VIII

. . . .

Scar and Ethan are mirror-images. In the scene where they finally meet, the confrontation is shot to emphasise this resemblance. Scar walks out of his tent. There is a close-up of Ethan, immediately followed by a close up of Scar, of a corresponding size and angle. Ethan walks up to Scar and stands very close. 'You speak pretty good American for a Comanch [sic]. Someone teach you?' Before they enter the tent, Scar will echo: 'You speak good Comanch. Someone teach you?' Inside, Scar shows Ethan the medal he had once given Debbie, and which Scar now wears around his own neck.[24]

For a white man, and one so hostile to Indians, Ethan is surprisingly familiar with Indian ways. Ethan is the one who first thinks the

Scar and Ethan are
mirror-images

Comanche might be on a murder raid, that driving off the cattle is just a feint. (Mose has suggested it is Indians, not rustlers – Mose who himself 'imitates' Indian ways with the feather in his hat, his funny little war dance when Ethan starts to unsaddle his horse, his war whoop later when the Comanche attack at the river.) In pursuit of the Comanche, the small band of Texans discover one of the Indians dead, buried under a stone in the traditional manner. Ethan shoots his eyes out, explaining that according to Indian religion, 'Ain't got no eyes he can't enter the spirit land, has to wander forever between the winds' (a little like Ethan himself, perhaps).[25] Ethan has Indian bead-work on his fringed rifle cover, and he recognises the singing of the chief's death song before the attack at the river. When Brad wonders if Indians are human, Ethan is the expert: 'Nope, a human rides a horse till it dies, then he goes on afoot. Comanch comes along, gets that horse up, rides him twenty more miles, then eats him.' Later he explains another difference to Marty: 'Injun'll chase a thing till he thinks he's chased it enough, then he quits. Same way when he runs, seems like he never learns there's such a thing as a critter'll just keep coming on.'

Ethan's act of scalping Scar is only the final confirmation that he has much of the Indian in him. The branch of the Comanche that Scar leads are called 'Nawyecka', which Ethan translates as 'goes about'; so they are wanderers, like Ethan himself. In *Regeneration Through Violence* Richard Slotkin traces the evolution during the eighteenth century of a particular type of American hero, based initially on a largely fictionalised Daniel Boone. Such a hero knows Indians intimately, has even lived among them. Like them he is at home in the wilderness, indeed has much of the wild in him, has the Indian virtues of hardiness and bravery, and is a skilled hunter. Such a type was developed by James Fenimore Cooper in his Leatherstocking Tales;[26] spiritually, his hero, Natty Bumppo, a man of the woods, has more in common with the Indians than with the whites.

But precisely because he is so close, he insists, like Ethan, on the difference. Bumppo refers to himself as 'a man without a cross', meaning that his blood-line is not crossed with that of the Indians. When Ethan first meets Marty, he too insists on racial difference: 'Fellow could mistake you for a half-breed.' Marty protests he is merely one-eighth Cherokee, but as far as Ethan is concerned that's enough. More than once he remarks that Marty is no kin to him, even though he has been adopted by Aaron and Martha.

IX

. . . .

A racist hero motivated by desire for his brother's wife; what kind of a Western is this? Aren't Westerns simple tales of good guys and bad guys? In fact by the mid-50s the Western had come a long way. In the early 30s the major studios had largely withdrawn from the genre, leaving the field to the smaller outfits of Poverty Row, or their own specialised B-feature units. But at the end of the decade Fox, Warners, Paramount, United Artists, even MGM, had resumed production of A-feature Westerns, and in the 40s came signs that the Western was ready to take on board the adult themes which film noir and the melodrama were exploring. *The Ox-Bow Incident* (1942) was a discomforting film about lynching. Howard Hughes' *The Outlaw*, released in 1943, was frank about sexual attraction, and King Vidor's *Duel in the Sun* (1946) was franker still. Raoul Walsh's *Pursued* (1947), often described as a noir Western, has some echoes of *The Searchers*: its hero (played by Robert Mitchum) is traumatised by the memory of his father's affair with his adopted mother, and has married his adopted sister. The quasi-incestuous nature of the relationship has, like Ethan's relation to Martha, a powerful charge.

The later 50s, the Eisenhower years, were times of peace and plenty in America. But Hollywood, its nose to the wind, sensed the tensions that seethed beneath the tranquil surface. In 1956 others besides Ford were at work dissecting the anatomy of the American family: Douglas Sirk with *Written on the Wind*, Nicholas Ray with *Bigger Than Life*, George Stevens with *Giant*, Elia Kazan with *Baby Doll*, all puncturing the complacency and hypocrisy of bourgeois life. Family and sexual tensions had become the motor driving many Western plots. In the extraordinary series of Westerns directed by Anthony Mann, most of which starred James Stewart, dysfunctional families are the norm. In *Winchester '73* (1950) Stewart seeks revenge on his brother, who has killed their father; in *The Man From Laramie* (1955) Stewart is caught up in a murderous feud between the two sons, one adopted, of a patriarchal rancher. And Western heroes, who once had been blameless paragons of courage and virtue, now revealed flaws. Stewart often displays a disturbed and violent character barely under control. In *The Last Hunt*, made the same year as *The Searchers*, Robert Taylor is a Civil War veteran and rabid Indian hater; like Ethan he kills buffalo just so that the Indians will starve.

X

....

The troubled hero may have been fashionable in the mid-50s Western, but Ethan is a difficult role to play. He is the pivotal character in the narrative; what Ethan will do is the question which keeps the audience hooked. But there's a grave risk of losing the audience if the character is too rebarbative.

John Wayne had just turned forty-eight when he began shooting *The Searchers*. Already he was wearing a hairpiece; 'welcome to the club,' he remarked to Harry Carey Jr when he saw him wearing his newly acquired toupee at the Monument Valley location.[27] It was Wayne's ninth starring role for John Ford; they went on to make a further five films together. It was Ford of course who had given him the chance to relaunch his career with *Stagecoach* in 1939, after the uncertain start of *The Big*

Trail (1930). In his book *John Wayne: The Politics of Celebrity* Garry Wills argues that at least half of the best films of each man were done when they were working together. With the possible exception of Henry Fonda (seven starring roles), no other leading actor was such a force in Ford's cinema (the early films with Harry Carey have mostly been lost, so we cannot make a judgement).

The relationship was close. Wayne was part of Ford's inner circle, the companion during many drinking bouts on board Ford's yacht, the *Araner*. Ford behaved to Wayne, as he behaved to all his intimates, with a mixture of bullying and banter. Yet somehow they all divined that his aggression towards them masked a deep affection he could not bring himself to reveal. For his part, Wayne regarded Ford with awe. In his letters to the director, full of talk about fishing and hunting trips, he always addresses Ford as 'coach'. He knew *Stagecoach* had saved him. As Harry Carey Jr says, Wayne 'never forgot what that movie had done for him and how Jack had fought to use him'.[28]

But what had Wayne done for Ford? It's commonly supposed that, unlike mere actors, film stars don't seek to impersonate characters. Instead, they are simply themselves. The sheer force and fascination of their personality overrides the local variations of the role. Certainly Wayne is a dominating presence on the screen, not just physically big but a figure of authority. His voice is loud and he speaks slowly, as if accustomed to being listened to. He brings to his roles, especially his Western roles, a massive assurance, an indomitable solidity. But it's not true that he simply performs himself, that his screen charisma is just a projection of his real-life persona. Ford used him in a variety of roles: as the naïve young hero of *Stagecoach*, as an officer mature beyond his years in *Fort Apache*, as a man of retirement age in *She Wore a Yellow Ribbon*, which Wayne himself considered his best role. Howard Hawks had been the first to draw out the iron in his soul, casting him as the obsessive Tom Dunson in *Red River* (1947). Ford expressed his admiration of Wayne's performance in that film with a characteristic put-down: 'I never knew the sonofabitch could act.'[29]

Wayne bestrides *The Searchers* like a colossus. It's not so much his size; Scar calls him 'Big Shoulders', but Garry Wills says the oft-repeated claims that Wayne was six foot four are exaggerated. When he walks along beside Jeffrey Hunter and Harry Carey Jr he's not appreciably taller than either, though Ford makes the most of his size by often putting the camera below head-height. It's Wayne's sheer presence that is so overwhelming. He can be very still, a hard thing to be on screen, and he gives the feeling of being relaxed, at ease with himself physically, whether seated in the rocking chair at the Edwards' ranch, leaning casually back on his bunk at the Jorgensens', or sprawling against his saddle while in camp with Marty and Look. Even in action his movements are usually calm and deliberate, as when he aims a careful shot at Scar from within the cave. When in the grip of his mania, frantically shooting fleeing Indians or slaughtering buffalo, his grace deserts him.

And then there's his voice, often caricatured, never surpassed among Western actors. In his first starring role in *The Big Trail* it was lightweight, high-pitched almost. A quarter of a century later it had matured into a firm baritone. Wisely he doesn't attempt a Texas accent, but he gives the salty dialogue, rich with the rhythms of biblical English and demotic American, the measured weight it deserves.[30]

Wayne's greatest acting in *The Searchers* is precisely at those moments when he has to do very little, when the audience has to intuit his feelings simply from his face. Ford's use of close-ups was the more telling for being so spare. The moment when Ethan looks back at his brother's ranch, imagining the horrors taking place there; a similar moment when he tops the ridge and sees the burning ranch below him; his expression after he has found the murdered body of Lucy and falls to the ground, stabbing at the earth with his knife; the agony on his face as the camera tracks in for a close-up as he watches the mad woman at the fort. In his face we see his loss, his suffering, all the more moving in that he can hardly express it in words, all the more affecting in one so strong. At such moments Wayne achieves the near-impossible, making us feel pity for such a monumentally self-sufficient figure, and sympathy for a murderous racist.

XI

. . . .

Wayne inhabits his space with confidence; but Ethan's restlessness is strongly marked in the composition of the film. Ford repeatedly favours a static camera position, from which he frames groups in formal poses carefully arranged across the screen, as in the opening scene as Ethan approaches his brother's farm, and now in the funeral scene. Ethan breaks up the ritual ('Put an amen to it'), rudely interrupting the singing of 'Shall

We Gather at the River', a sacrosanct Fordian anthem which he will again disrupt at the wedding of Laurie and Charlie. He charges out of the frame at the bottom left corner, the remaining mourners trailing in his wake.

As we dissolve to the next shot, Ethan intrudes, walking rapidly across the front of the frame, so close that he's not even in focus. The Jorgensens, rooted to the spot, watch him. In the next shot Mrs Jorgensen pleads with him not to waste lives in vengeance, but he's not listening. We cut back to Mr Jorgensen and Laurie, who is saying goodbye to Marty. As Marty rides out of frame to follow Ethan, the camera moves sideways to take in Mrs Jorgensen too, and then Laurie takes up her place between her parents, in a composed tableau of those who are left behind.

Hard on the trail of the Comanche, Ethan is confrontational with his fellows, refusing to let Marty call him uncle ('no, nor Methuselah neither'), questioning the competence of Clayton, who already suspects that Ethan is less interested in finding the girls alive than in vengeance. Out in open country the little band of Rangers find themselves flanked by columns of Indians on both sides. The Comanche ride along the skyline, following the rise and fall of the terrain as if they are part of it, at one with the landscape. At their backs is a huge mass of stone called Square Rock, on the western side of Monument Valley. Ford had used it for another confrontation with Indians, when Captain Thursday meets Cochise in *Fort Apache*.

The Rangers take refuge across the river. In this desert land, water has an almost biblical symbolism. Peter Wollen has pointed to the importance in Ford's work of the desert/garden antinomy which Henry Nash Smith identified as central to nineteenth-century discourses about the West.[31] Its most poignant representation is the cactus rose which John Wayne hands Vera Miles in *The Man Who Shot Liberty Valance*. There's nothing much that could be called a garden in *The Searchers*, and indeed one wonders how anyone could be trying to farm in such a place. But at significant moments water, the sine qua non of cultivation, irrigates the parched earth. When after many weary months Ethan and Marty return to the Jorgensens' ranch, there is a lyrical shot of horses gambolling in a water hole. When they make contact with Debbie, she runs to them across a small stream cutting through the desert sand. Trapped in a cave, with Ethan sorely wounded, Marty finds water dripping from a rock. And when at last they bring Debbie back home to the Jorgensens', horses are once again contentedly nuzzling a pool of water.

As the Rangers make a stand at the river we get our second sight of Scar, briefly glimpsed prior to the attack on the Edwards' ranch. He's played by Henry Brandon. Born Heinrich von Kleinbach in Berlin, Brandon specialised in villainous roles, often racially threatening (he played Fu Manchu, for example). He is certainly an imposing figure, but it has to be said there's nothing very Indian about his looks. Ford usually cast Navajo, residents of Monument Valley, as the spear-carriers in his films, but for Indians with speaking roles he almost invariably preferred white actors, as was then the custom of Hollywood.[32]

The Comanche charge is beaten off; as so often in the Western, the Indians fight with more bravado than tactical nous. Ethan continues firing as they retreat, until the Reverend Clayton physically restrains him. As befits a frontier preacher, Clayton, though as ready to fight as the next man when the heat of battle is on, is mindful of the proprieties: 'Let them carry off their hurt and dead.' There's a firm distinction drawn between Christian decency and Ethan's uncivilised blood-lust, though religion in Ford is never confused with piousness; the preacher in *My Darling Clementine* has 'read the good book from cover to cover and back again' and 'nary found one word agin dancing', and Clayton will preside over dancing and drinking at Laurie's wedding. His priestly office does not escape the mockery of Mose, who jokes 'I been baptised, Reverend' when asked how far it is to the river.

Disgusted with Clayton's interference in his personal vendetta against the Indians, Ethan vows he will pursue them alone. Marty and Brad insist that they will go too. Along the trail they notice some of the Indians have detoured into a narrow canyon. Ethan goes to investigate. When he comes back he seems preoccupied, disturbed. He sits and digs viciously with his knife in the sand between his legs. Brad and Marty ask what's up but they get no coherent response, though Marty notices Ethan's 'Johnny Reb' coat has disappeared. Later, it is twilight. Brad comes excitedly into camp saying he's seen Lucy. Ethan, his voice quiet with emotion, says it wasn't Lucy, but 'a buck' wearing Lucy's dress. Tenderly he explains that he found Lucy dead back in the canyon and buried her in his coat. Brad has to know the details: 'Did they …? Was she …?' Ethan blazes into anger at the boy's clumsy attempt to uncover what Ethan has tried to put underground. 'Whaddaya want me to do, draw ya a picture? Spell it out? Don't ever ask me, long as you live, don't ever ask me more.'

The most heart-wrenching scenes in Ford are when the emotion is only half expressed. 'Heard melodies are sweet, but those unheard/Are sweeter,' Keats wrote. Ford knew the same applied to moments of anguish. It's extraordinary how many moments of violence are suppressed. We don't see the Indian attack on the Edwards' ranch. We see neither Lucy's death nor Brad's. We don't see Look killed, only her dead body. Even the shooting of Futterman and his accomplices takes places in semi-darkness. We feel the horror of Lucy's death all the more because our imagination has to supply what Ethan will not tell, or in the case of Martha's death, will not let Marty see. At the same time, keeping such things hidden not only invests them with extraordinary emotive power. It also allows the film to hint at the darkness deep in Ethan. He justifies keeping Lucy's fate a secret on the grounds of sparing Brad's feelings. But he turns off the trail to penetrate a narrow crevice in the rocks, and when he emerges his savage stabbing with his knife seems to mimic a violent sexual act, drawing us 'a picture' of the act of rape which obsesses him.[33] Only Scar's death and mutilation are seen on screen. It's as if at the end suppression is no longer possible. Things must finally be brought to light, after which there can be resolution.

XII

. . . .

A volley of gunshots signals Brad's death as, distraught with grief, he rushes into the Comanche camp. The camera holds on the faces of Ethan and Marty, absorbing yet more tragedy, before dissolving to a beautiful shot of Ethan and Marty riding diagonally left to right across the vastness of Monument Valley. It's dusk, or early morning, and half the valley is obscured in mist, while a soft autumnal light bathes the scene. There's another dissolve to a shot of them riding in the other direction, across a field of snow, and then another to a shot of Marty and Ethan in some trees. It's striking just how many scenes in the film are linked by dissolves, the traditional signal of time passing. The two shots also connote distance – the emptiness of the space they traverse, going first one way then another. On the soundtrack we hear a musical phrase from the opening song: 'ride away'.

Time and place. Both the chronology and the geography of *The Searchers* are relative, stretching and contracting elusively. How long does the action of the film last? And where exactly do Marty and Ethan search? 'Texas 1868', the screen says at the beginning. At that time Debbie is, we suppose, eight or nine. Lana Wood, who plays her as a young girl, was nine at the time the film was shot (though the script says Debbie is eleven; the original novel 'pushing ten'). Her sister Natalie Wood, who plays the older Debbie, was seventeen. On this basis, then, the action of the film lasts eight years, concluding in 1876. A document entitled 'Route Traveled by The Searchers' in the Ford collection at the Lilly Library summarises the chronology and geography of the story from Alan LeMay's novel. It begins later, in the fall of 1870, and ends 'Winter 1876–7'.

From internal evidence, the total duration seems to be less than this, though the film often seems deliberately vague. We can assume that not much time elapses between the Comanche raid on the Edwards' ranch and the point at which Ethan, Marty and Brad catch up with the Comanche, the episode which ends with Brad's death. The two shots which follow of Ethan and Marty roaming mark an ellipsis, but one of indeterminate length. Sitting on his horse as the snow falls, marking the passing of the seasons, Ethan remarks that they will find Debbie, 'sure as the turning of the earth', a time-reference that might suggest passing days, months, years. But how many?

When Ethan and Marty return, Mr Jorgensen says it's a year since he got Ethan's letter telling of Brad's death (though we don't know how long the letter may have taken to arrive). Immediately they set off again to find Futterman, the trader who has news of Debbie. Subsequent events are recounted in Marty's letter to Laurie, but how long they take and how much time has elapsed from writing this letter to its delivery is also hard to say. Not as much as one might think, presumably, since Jorgensen is delighted to get 'two letters in one year, by golly!' (actually there have been three if we count the one from Futterman). We have to assume that a much lengthier passage of time, several years, elapses between the events described in the letter to Laurie, and Ethan and Marty's appearance down on the border, where they find Scar's camp. Just before he takes an Indian arrow Ethan says Scar has got to kill them: 'we've been asking for it for five years.' He is severely wounded, but by the time Ethan and Marty arrive back at the Jorgensens' there has been time for his wound to heal, and for Laurie to decide that she can no longer wait for Marty – although when we see Debbie the second time, when she is rescued, she is wearing the same clothes as the first time, which might suggest the time elapsed is not so great after all. Laurie protests to Marty when he returns the second time that she has had only one letter from him in five years. If she means five years since he first left, that appears to confirm Ethan's estimate of the total time they have been searching.

Geography is also somewhat vague. In terms of the film's actual location, Ethan's journey is circular. At the beginning we see him coming out of the valley towards his brother's house in Monument Valley; at the end the door of the Jorgensens', also in Monument Valley, closes upon him. Location scenes shot outside the Valley are few. A second unit went to Gunnison in Colorado to shoot snow scenes for three days at the end of February 1955. The scene where Ethan shoots the buffalo was filmed soon after in Elk Island National Park, near Edmonton, Alberta, Canada. The scenes shot on a sound stage were done at the RKO-Pathé studio from 18 July till 13 August 1955. These included not only such obvious interiors as the inside of the Edwards' and Jorgensens' houses, but the brief scene with the Rangers in the marsh, the shooting of Futterman, and the scene in the snow where Ethan says they'll find Debbie 'sure as the turning of the earth'. However, the Monument Valley locations are real enough. The company shot there for a whole month, from 16 June till 10 July 1955, about the hottest time of the year.

Apart from these excursions, the entire search, for five years or more, is shot in the Valley, a location which measures about thirty miles by forty. The diegetic space is much vaster. After the opening title 'Texas 1868' there are no subsequent captions to indicate place, but scraps of dialogue give an occasional indication. When Ethan first returns to the Jorgensens' he says they have been to 'Fort Richardson, Wingate, Cobb, Anadarko Agency'. This would represent a considerable journey. We do not know exactly where in the very large state of Texas the Edwards' farm is supposed to be, but presumably out on the frontier, somewhere in the western part. Fort Richardson was in northern Texas, not far to the west of the present Dallas-Fort Worth conurbation. Fort Wingate was in New Mexico, on the other side of Albuquerque, a distance of six or seven hundred miles to the west. Fort Cobb and the Anadarko Indian Agency were back the other way, in Oklahoma, or what was then Indian Territory, over two hundred miles east of Fort Richardson. So their search extends, there and back, for a distance of nigh on two thousand miles.

There are few other precise geographical locations mentioned in the film though there are plenty in LeMay's novel. We don't know where Futterman's trading post is, nor exactly where we are when Ethan first meets Scar, except that it's obviously deep into the Hispanic regions of the Southwest, near or even over the border. When they catch up with Scar at the end he is at 'Seven Fingers of Brazos', at the 'south end of the Malapai'. The Brazos river runs across the north-west part of Texas, but that's an awful lot of country. The geographical vagueness has the effect of increasing our sense of the vast distances Ethan and Marty must travel in their search, just as the imprecision of the duration expended makes time hang heavy upon them.

XIII
....

Following the shot in the snow, there's another dissolve, more time passing, to a distant shot of Ethan and Marty approaching the Jorgensens' ranch. It's a pastoral scene of great but simple beauty; of all Hollywood's legendary one-eyed directors (Fritz Lang, Raoul Walsh, André de Toth), Ford surely had the best sense of composition. As horses wallow in a pool of water, a cowboy, whom Ethan and Marty greet as Sam, stands beside a corral coiling a length of rope. Mrs Jorgensen is seen, as Martha was, from inside her house, moving outside to greet the riders. Lars Jorgensen comes to stand alongside her, like Aaron. In a reverse shot, we see Laurie take up her position screen right as the third point of the little triangular family, framed against their Texas Gothic-style ranch house.[34] Ethan asks Mr Jorgensen if he got the letter about Brad. Jorgensen says he did, shakes Ethan's hand and gestures, nearly in tears, at the wide open space around them. 'Oh, Ethan, this country. ....'; not for the first time, words fail.

Inside the house Laurie carries water for Marty to have a bath. Scenes of men bathing are frequent and significant in the Western. The male body, usually encased in its armour of rough denim, leather chaps, gunbelt and boots, is only exposed when wounded (as Ethan will later be), or when undergoing the cleansing ritual that marks the passage from wilderness to civilisation, across the frontier which Western heroes bestride. (Sam Peckinpah, in so many ways the inheritor of Ford's mantle, was obsessed with such scenes, including them in *Ride the High*

A composed tableau of those who are left behind

A pastoral scene of great but simple beauty

Finale: on the Jorgensens' porch

After finding Lucy, Ethan stabs savagely with his knife

Wayne as Ethan: the agony on his face

The audience has to intuit his feelings

Monument Valley: the splendour of its vistas

The Comanche: at one with the landscape

Magical scenery: Totem Pole

The Jorgensens' house: Texas Gothic

Reading Marty's letter

Look, or Wild Goose Flying in the Night Sky (Beulah Archuletta)

The camera is positioned in a place of refuge, a dark-womb like space

Laurie and Charlie: 'Skip to my Lou'

'The sun's low down the sky, Lorena'

Real Indian life'? Natalie Wood as Debbie

South of the border …

… down Mexico way

Ethan with Scar's scalp

'Do you know what Ethan will do if he has a chance? Put a bullet in her brain.'

Ethan's gesture

'Let's go home, Debbie.'

Country, *Major Dundee*, *The Wild Bunch*, *The Ballad of Cable Hogue* and *Pat Garrett & Billy the Kid*, besides two films he scripted but did not direct, *The Glory Guys* and *Villa Rides*.)

'Oh, Ethan, this country. ...' Texas 1868: we've seen the significance of the date, just after the Civil War; what of the place? General Phil Sheridan memorably remarked that if he owned hell and Texas, he'd live in hell and rent out Texas. It's a tough place to pioneer in. Aaron tells his brother that some of his neighbours have quit, going back to 'chopping cotton' (in the more settled east of the state, presumably). Later, Mrs Jorgensen describes the character of the people: 'A Texican is nothing but a human man way out on a limb ...This year and next ... and maybe for a hundred more. But I don't think it'll be for ever. Some day this country's going to be a fine good place to be. Maybe it needs our bones in the ground before that time can come.' Texas occupies a pivotal position in the mythical geography of the Western; but not as an actual location. In a survey, two French academics sampled 411 Westerns, and in 19% the story was set in Texas. Yet the actual number of films which actually used Texas as a location was tiny.[35] Why? Because most of Texas doesn't look like Texas ought to. Fixed in our minds is an image of canyons and mesas, an image derived largely from the movies themselves. In fact much of Texas, the east and the north, is flat, almost featureless, yielding little of interest to the camera; though good cattle country. The landscape we see in *The Searchers*, by contrast – Monument Valley, Arizona – satisfies our aesthetic expectation but is an improbable place to raise cattle, as Jorgensen is trying to do ('next time I'll raise pigs, by golly!').[36]

Mrs Jorgensen's feisty speech about Texas is the only direct expression in the film of the ideology that underpins the Western myth, that of Manifest Destiny, the idea that the expansion of those of European origins into the American West was both inevitable and desirable, a natural outcome of a historical process. As the first frame of the credits inform us, *The Searchers* is a C.V.Whitney picture. Whitney's involvement with the film was primarily a financial one, but in a letter written while the film was in preparation Whitney ventured to offer Ford some advice about the film's content.[37] He wanted the film to have a more portentous message. The market was being flooded with Westerns, and so there was a need to 'dignify or broaden the story' by changing the title to *The Searchers for Freedom* and adding a prologue and epilogue 'in order to strengthen the ideas behind the new title and to emphasise *The American Theme or Story*. Do I make myself clear?' But Ford was notoriously deaf to advice he didn't care to hear, and there's no evidence that he took any notice.

Polo-playing Cornelius Vanderbilt 'Sonny' Whitney was the cousin of John Hay 'Jock' Whitney. Both were wealthy and well-connected, the scions of industrial dynasties with extensive interests in mining. Jock became American ambassador to Britain.[38] Sonny had a 'good war', as they say, winning the Distinguished Service Medal, and afterwards was Assistant Secretary of the Air Force under Harry Truman. Society figures, sportsmen and entrepreneurs, the Whitneys dabbled in film production, both having a financial involvement in David O. Selznick's *Gone with the Wind*. In his autobiography, *High Peaks*, published in 1977, C.V.Whitney recounts how an interest in the West had been formed at an early age, when he was taken to see Buffalo Bill Cody's Wild West in Madison Square Garden.[39] C.V.Whitney Pictures were to film two other pieces of Americana the year after *The Searchers*: *The Missouri Traveler* and *The Young Land*, both produced by Patrick Ford, with the latter starring Pat Wayne. But they made little impression and the company was wound up in December 1959.

The Searchers was not one of the career peaks Sonny saw fit to record in his book. But Whitney and his wife did visit Monument Valley while the film was in production. The *Film Daily* reported their visit with photographs in its issue of 20 March 1956, and in his autobiography, *Fall Guy*, Chuck Roberson says Ford ordered him to stage a fistfight at dinner in front of the astonished Whitneys, as a practical joke. The gossip column of the *New York Journal* dated 14 October 1955 recounts that 'Sonny makes a fleeting appearance as a hard-hitting US cavalryman in *The Search* [sic] when star John Wayne leads a charge on a band of pesky redskins', though whether his appearance survived the cutting room must await the verdict of a sharper-eyed scholar.[40]

Whitney's involvement with Selznick came about through his friendship with Merian C. Cooper, who in the mid-30s had persuaded him to participate in Pioneer Pictures, formed to make prestige films in the newly perfected Technicolor process. Pioneer was eventually merged with Selznick International. Cooper was a man whose early life would have made a stirring movie in itself, with the intrepid hero perhaps played by Clark Gable. Having fought with the National Guard against Pancho

Villa, Cooper became a pilot in World War I and was shot down and imprisoned by the Germans. After the war he flew for the Polish Air Force against the Bolsheviks, and was shot down again. Imprisoned this time by the Russians, he escaped and made his way to Warsaw, where he was decorated by the Polish leader, Pilsudski. In the 20s he was a newspaperman before making documentary films with Ernest Schoedsack in such exotic spots as Ethiopia, Iran and Thailand, also finding time to help pioneer Pan American Airways. In 1933 he and Schoedsack directed *King Kong* for RKO, before Cooper succeeded Selznick as head of production at the studio. At RKO Cooper formed a close working relationship with John Ford, and later in the decade he tried to persuade Selznick to back *Stagecoach*. Selznick turned up his nose, calling it 'just another Western'. After the war Cooper and Ford together formed Argosy Pictures, and prior to *The Searchers* Cooper had been co-producer with Ford on eight films in as many years, including five Westerns: *3 Godfathers*, *Wagon Master* and the 'cavalry trilogy' of *Fort Apache*, *She Wore a Yellow Ribbon*, and *Rio Grande*.

Old soldiers all, Ford, Cooper and Whitney shared a fascination with the military. According to Dan Ford, C.V.Whitney had originally wanted to work with Ford on a picture to be called *The Valiant Virginians*, based on Civil War stories by James Warner Bellah, whose work had formed the basis of the cavalry trilogy.[41] Cooper thought that a good solid Western with John Wayne would be a better bet for the fledgling C.V.Whitney Pictures. Accordingly, he optioned a story that had begun to appear in the *Saturday Evening Post* in November 1954. Entitled 'The Avenging Texans', it was written by Alan LeMay. Retitled as *The Searchers*, it was published as a novel at the end of 1954.

Born in Indianapolis in 1899, LeMay published some Western novels in the later 20s and 30s, as well as numerous stories, mostly in *Collier's* magazine. In 1940 he became a screenwriter, working on *North West Mounted Police* and other films for Cecil B. DeMille. His achievements in the movies were modest, though he was something of a Western specialist; writing credits included *San Antonio* (1945), with Errol Flynn, and *Cheyenne* (1947), directed by Raoul Walsh. He produced a couple of films and directed one, the Western *High Lonesome*, made from his own script in 1950. LeMay remains much better known for two novels which others made into films: *The Searchers*, and *The Unforgiven*, a kind of captivity narrative in reverse, filmed in 1960 by

John Huston with Audrey Hepburn as an Indian girl brought up with a white family. Violence erupts when her Kiowa kinfolk come to take her back.

XIV
. . . .

Ford's choice of scriptwriter for *The Searchers* was Frank Nugent. Originally the movie critic of the *New York Times*, he'd written an enthusiastic review of *Stagecoach*, calling it 'a motion picture that sings a song of camera'. During the early 40s Nugent was hired by Darryl Zanuck at 20th Century-Fox as a script-doctor, and there he first met Ford. In 1947 Nugent had written a profile of Ford for the *Saturday Evening Post*. He told Lindsay Anderson how he came to write scripts:

> After the article was finished I dropped in to see him one day and he started talking about a picture he had in mind. 'The Cavalry. In all westerns the Cavalry rides in to the rescue of the beleaguered wagon train or whatever, and then it rides off again. I've been thinking about it – what it was like at a Cavalry post, remote, people with their own personal problems, over everything the threat of Indians, of death. ...' I said it sounded great. And then he knocked me right off my seat by asking how I'd like to write it for him. When I stumbled and stammered he grinned and said it would be fun. He gave me a list of about 50 books to read – memoirs, novels, anything about the period. Later he sent me down into the Old Apache country to nose around. ... When I got back Ford asked me if I thought I had enough research. I said yes. 'Good,' he said. 'Now just forget everything you've read and we'll start writing a movie.' [42]

Nugent went on to write eleven films for Ford in all, including some of his most personal works such as *Wagon Master* and *The Quiet Man*. He told Lindsay Anderson: 'Ford works very, very closely with the writer or writers. I don't think it would be entirely true to say that he sees the story in its entirety when he begins – although he sometimes pretends to. Sometimes he is groping, like a musician who has a theme but doesn't quite know how to develop it. ... He has a wonderful ear for dialogue and a lot of it is his own.'

LeMay's novel wasn't holy writ; Nugent made a number of significant changes, and some minor ones. Originally, the hero was named Amos Edwards; his name was changed apparently because of its comic association with the popular radio show *Amos 'n' Andy*.[43] In the novel, though Amos is in love with his brother's wife neither she nor her husband is aware of this. Marty is not part-Indian. Amos does not have a mysterious or shady past. And instead of bringing Debbie home, Amos is killed by a Comanche woman during an attack on their camp. It's left to Marty to rescue Debbie, and the implication is that he will eventually marry her; in the book Laurie does not wait for him. There's some amalgamation of characters: in the book there are two Indian chiefs, Bluebonnet and Scar; there is a character named Mose Harper in the book, but Mose in the film is more like the novel's character of Lige Powers, an aged buffalo hunter. Clayton is largely an invention of the film.

Most of the memorable lines in the film are in the script, though there's no way of telling whether they originated with Ford or Nugent, and some are in the original novel – for example Clayton's speech to the young Lieutenant Greenhill before the attack on the Comanche village (given to a character named Clinton in the book): 'And don't pay them Comanches no mind, neither – just keep your eye on me. I'm the hard case you're up against around here, not them childish savages. If you don't hear me first time I holler, you better by God read my mind – I don't aim to raise no two hollers on any one subject in hand.'[44]

There are actions which are not detailed in the script and which we may assume Ford himself created on the set. Look for example at the sequence when Ethan and Marty return to the Jorgensens' a year or so after the death of Brad. Marty's bath is scripted;[45] but not Laurie throwing water over him after he thinks she's left the room, an action which expresses both the youthful high spirits of the couple in contrast to the gravitas of Ethan, and the extent to which Laurie is the one who makes all the running in the relationship. The Jorgensen women are indeed formidable; they give at least as good as they get. Mrs Jorgensen's speech about the future of Texas is in the script, but not her putting away the liquor jug with a firmness that brooks no argument, telling the men it's time for bed; nor is her husband's comment, as if in explanation of her bossiness, that 'she used to be a schoolteacher, you know'. That remark does come later in the script (and is repeated in the film), but not as a piece of comedy, simply an explanation of why she is a good reader. Similarly, the business of Mr Jorgensen putting on his spectacles when Ethan reads Futterman's letter has been added, though in the script (and in the film) he performs the same act when Laurie later reads Marty's letter. Ford was never reluctant to repeat a joke if it was good enough.

Several other bits of business are added to the sequence at the Jorgensens'. As Marty and Ethan prepare for bed, Laurie comes to say goodnight. In the script:

JORGENSEN'S VOICE
(calling)
Laurie! … Come … come!
Ethan opens the door, enters.
LAURIE
Yes, Pa! Good night Martie [sic] …
Good night, Mister Edwards …
She wants to kiss Martie but is shy in Ethan's presence and hurries out.
MARTIN
Good night … Laurie …
ETHAN
Good night …

In the film, when she is called out of the room by her father, Laurie moves away from Marty towards the door, her back to us as she passes Ethan. She looks across at him, then, plucking up courage, she suddenly turns back and plants a kiss on Marty's mouth. Now, when she moves back towards the door, there is a firmness to her step, and as she passes Ethan again she looks at him with a confident nod of her head and says, 'Good night Mr Edwards', as if to say 'I don't mind if you did see me kiss him.' Ethan is amused, and says not merely 'good night', but 'good night, *Miss* Jorgensen', the mock formality a tribute to her boldness.

Ford has often been found wanting in his depiction of sexual relations.[46] But there is considerable delicacy in the scenes between Marty and Laurie, which capture the awkward and hesitant emotions of those for whom deep feelings are not often or easily expressed. The next day Laurie is in her apron when Marty appears.[47] She asks him if he slept well. Awkwardly he edges towards her, then suddenly grabs her in a stiff embrace and kisses her. Delighted at finally eliciting such a positive response, she kisses him back enthusiastically, then stands over him, eyes shining: 'I'll get your coffee.'

> Marty: You know Laurie, I was just thinking, it's about time you and me started going steady, huh?
> Laurie (drawing herself up to her full height): Well, Martin Pawley, you and me been going steady since we was three years old.
> Marty: We have?
> Laurie: 'Bout time you found out about it.
> Marty: Well, gosh, Laurie, I've always been fond of you but, well, what with all this trouble with Debbie and Ethan …

None of this is in the script. The film shows a nice contrast between Marty's firmness in the face of Ethan's murderous intentions towards Debbie, and his bashfulness in love. Laurie next, as in the script, gives him the letter from Futterman. What is added is Marty's near-illiteracy, as he stumbles to make out the words (this lack of schooling will again be brought to our attention when he reads out Ethan's will). It shows him as the junior partner in the relationship with Laurie; but this is contrasted with the relative moral stature of the two. Marty may be gauche, ill-educated, little versed in affairs of the heart; but he is the still moral centre of the film, the one who, while all around him are driven by their prejudices, sees clearly that Debbie can and must be saved. There is a powerful irony in the fact that Marty is the one person in the film of mixed race, a 'half-breed' in Ethan's casually insulting term; worth considering when charges of racism are thrown at Ford – or at the Western generally.

Laurie grabs the letter from him and completes reading it. Her impatience is a cover for the powerful emotions she is struggling to control, at the realisation that Marty, whom she believes has come back to her for good, is determined to set off after Ethan. Heartbroken that Marty puts his care for his adopted sister before his feelings for her, she masks her emotion in exasperation, finally pushing him back over the settle. The action is both comic and moving. Like Shakespeare, Ford loved the mixture of emotions, the sheer complexity of response achieved by mingling comedy with pathos or tragedy. There's another example at the end of the film, in which the killing of Scar and the rescue of Debbie is immediately followed by broad comedy, the Reverend Clayton being tended for a wound in his backside caused by the inexpertly wielded sword of the young army lieutenant.[48] The scene between Marty and Laurie concludes, much as in the script, with Laurie giving Marty her horse to chase after Ethan, while, in tears, she tells him she can't promise to wait any longer. 'I ain't cut out to be no old maid' – a threat which she makes good by accepting Charlie McCorry's proposal before Marty can return.

The scene ends on a close-up of Laurie leaning on the hitching rail weeping as Marty gallops past her. It's an affecting performance by Vera Miles, who soon after was contracted by Alfred Hitchcock for *The Wrong Man*. When she got pregnant by her new husband, former 'Tarzan' Gordon Scott, Hitchcock was enraged that she hadn't saved herself for his next picture, *Vertigo*. It seems Hitchcock never forgave her, relegating her to the minor role of Janet Leigh's sister in *Psycho* as a punishment.[49] Ford, however, had no such difficulties, and gave her another excellent part in *The Man Who Shot Liberty Valance*, in which she once again plays John Qualen's daughter.

XV

. . . .

While a script was being prepared, Cooper attempted to set up a deal with one of the major studios. C.V.Whitney Pictures would put up some of the production finance, the studio would put up the rest, would distribute the film and then split the proceeds. It was a common enough arrangement by the mid-50s, when the studios' previously total grip on all aspects of picture-making had been loosened by the rise of so-called independent production, in which established stars and other talent manoeuvred to change their status as salaried employees and cut themselves a slice of the profits. There were negotiations with Columbia, for whom the previous year Ford had made *The Long Gray Line*. In a memo Cooper sent to Columbia he proposed that if Whitney paid production costs, estimated at $2,200,000, all rentals on the picture would go to C.V.Whitney Pictures until production costs were paid off; then, after Columbia's distribution costs had been paid, 25% of further rentals would go to Columbia, and 75% to Whitney up to a gross of $5,000,000, after which Columbia's share would climb to 30%. An alternative deal could be that Columbia paid all production costs, then after recouping these costs and another $850,000 for distribution, revenues would be split 50:50. Harry Cohn, head of Columbia, sent a rather pained cable, complaining that Whitney seemed to want to get his money out first. Cooper, to use the title of a 50s Columbia picture, wasn't Born Yesterday. In the event, Warner Bros. offered what Columbia were reluctant to concede, a deal in which Whitney was guaranteed to get his money back. Whitney would meet all the costs of production, but as soon as the negative was handed over Warners would reimburse the full cost, up to $2,500,000. Warners agreed to spend at least $500,000 on 'advertising and exploitation'. Once gross receipts topped $5,000,000 they were to be split 50:50. It was written into the distribution agreement that John Wayne would receive 10% of gross receipts, and was to receive an advance of $250,000. According to Dan Ford, Ford himself was to receive a flat fee of $125,000 plus 10% of the net.[50]

XVI

. . . .

The letter Jorgensen gives Ethan is from a trader named Jerem Futterman, who encloses a scrap of calico that Mrs Jorgensen confirms is from Debbie's apron. Ethan, with Marty in pursuit, goes to seek out Futterman. The trader is a suspicious-looking character who is greedy for Ethan's money. Later that night, Futterman and friends attempt to ambush Ethan and Marty (on a set rather too obviously constructed in the studio). Ethan is too smart for them; not overly concerned with legal niceties, he shoots them all in the back as they try to run away. (At the end of the film the Reverend Clayton, still suspicious which side of the law Ethan operates on, tells him there's a charge against him relating to Futterman's death. The issue is never resolved, since Lieutenant Greenhill bursts in with Mose, who has information on Scar's whereabouts.)

Immediately after the death of Futterman, Charlie McCorry arrives at the Jorgensens' with a letter, from Marty to Laurie. Marty, his literacy not improved, has misspelled her name as Laury (the envelope she holds in her hand appears to be optimistically addressed 'Laury Jorgensen, Texas'). As Laurie reads out loud, we have a flashback to the scenes the letter recounts, an unusual strategy in the Western, which usually favours more direct narrative methods. At this point the narration is complex. As Tag Gallagher has observed, not only do we get Laurie's reading of Marty's account of Ethan's actions, which he clearly has trouble making sense of. As the audience of the scene, we are presented both with Laurie's response to this (which includes several heartfelt recriminations on Marty's apparent indifference to her feelings – 'Just how old does he think I am?!'), and the varying reactions of those who are listening to her: her father and mother, and Charlie.[51]

Charlie McCorry is a strange creation. His exaggeratedly hick accent and quaint vocabulary ('I'll thank you to unhand my fiancée') make him a figure of fun. Ken Curtis, who plays the role, was a member of Ford's inner circle, married to his daughter, Barbara, and a member of The Sons of the Pioneers singing group, appearing on screen with them in *Rio Grande*. Harry Carey Jr describes the accent Curtis uses as 'Colorado dryland'.[52] Ford heard him using it in fun on the set and liked it so much he demanded he play the role that way, countering Curtis' protests with the argument that it would get him noticed in the thankless role of the guy who doesn't get the girl. It seems to have worked, since Carey says it helped Curtis land the role of Festus in the long-running TV Western series *Gunsmoke*. But the accent makes it hard to take Charlie seriously as a suitor to Laurie. Would she really rather have this gormless bumpkin than wait for Marty? If so it makes Laurie less sympathetic than she otherwise appears; though it is Laurie who has the most explicitly racist speech in the entire film. When Marty says he must go and fetch Debbie home, she retorts: 'Fetch what home? The leavings a Comanche buck sold time and again to the highest bidder, with savage brats of her own? ... Do you know what Ethan will do if he has a chance? Put a bullet in her brain. I tell you, Martha would want him to.'[53]

Throughout the picture Marty, in Jeffrey Hunter's unselfish and sympathetic performance, represents the voice of decency, the standard against which Ethan's actions are judged. Ridiculed, undermined, constantly cut down to size as young men usually are in the Western (Ethan variously calls him blanket-head or chunk-head), he doggedly persists in his mission, not just to find Debbie but to rescue her from Ethan's murderous intent. For most of the film's length, Marty has a clear-sighted view of Ethan. But in his letter to Laurie Marty describes, and we actually see, a disturbing and uncomfortable occurrence. In flashback, as Laurie reads the letter, Marty attempts to trade with some Comanche. He believes that in exchange for two blue silk rosettes ('Lard type hog') and a hat for her father, he has bought a blanket from a stout, beaming Indian woman. Only when she trails after him does he realise he has purchased her as a wife. Ethan regards the episode as a huge joke, a further opportunity to humiliate Marty. Laurie takes it as a deliberate insult to herself, that Marty should marry an Indian instead of her, and throws his letter in the fire. Like Ethan, her father and Charlie McCorry are also hugely amused, Charlie seeing an opportunity to pursue his own suit, encouraged by Laurie's father ('A man should get married early in life, right, Mama?').

For Charlie and Mr Jorgensen, it's simply funny that Marty has 'married' an Indian woman. But why is Ethan able to make a joke of it, when he regards Debbie's union with an Indian with such revulsion? Doubtless because to a patriarchal society an Indian man marrying a white woman is more threatening. But it's surely also because the woman he laughingly refers to as 'Mrs Pawley' is plump and homely. She's not a challenge, she's just not plausible as a sexual partner, and when after they have made camp she dutifully lies down beside Marty, he literally kicks her out of bed. Were she an exotically sexualised Indian maiden such as the one James Stewart falls for in *Broken Arrow* (played, of course, by a white actress, Debra Paget), Marty's discomfiture would not be nearly so great: but doubtless Ethan's would be greater.[54]

It's a good question whether we, the audience, are supposed to guffaw along with Ethan as Marty's foot propels his 'wife' down the side of the hill.[55] Perhaps; no one has yet claimed Ford as prematurely politically correct. One has a sneaking suspicion that we're meant to find her physical attributes funny in themselves. And yet she is the one Indian character who is given any sort of individuality (Scar is barely more than a stereotype). She is good-natured to a fault, making coffee, willing to take on whatever identity Marty requires, even to the extent of changing her name. Mistaking Marty's expostulatory 'Look' as a vocative, she replies in Comanche that if he wishes to call her that it's fine. (Ethan with a sneer translates, giving her Comanche name as 'Wild Goose, Flying in the Night Sky'; how could such a plain girl have such a fancy name, he implies.) So some groundwork is established for a more caring response, and if we do indeed succumb to Ethan's coarse laughter, we are soon sorry for it. So is Ethan himself. Terrified by their attempt to press her for information about Scar, 'Look' deserts, but leaves an arrow of stones to indicate her direction. Following, Ethan and Marty eventually catch up with her – too late. In an Indian village attacked by the Seventh Cavalry they find her body. 'It's Look,' says Ethan, with real tenderness in his voice. 'What did those soldiers have to go and kill her for, Ethan?' exclaims Marty. 'She never done nobody any harm.' Exactly so.

XVII
. . . .

The sequence which follows is significantly different from Frank Nugent's script, which had earlier received some forceful input from Ford himself, in a series of memos. In the film, Ethan and Marty arrive at the fort and are shown some white captives who have been rescued from the Indians during the cavalry attack. In the script, before they see the captives Ethan and Marty intrude on the general in charge, who is boasting of his victory to some journalists.[56] The general is not named in the script, but a memo from Ford dated 26 January 1955 identifies him: 'As to General Custer. Make him an arrogant, colorful character. ... Custer should be in a magnificent army overcoat ... Fur collar ... gold braid ... should wear a small sealskin cap ala [sic] a Russian Grand Duke ... whose present it was.' Another note (15 February 1955) calls him 'an arrogant phoney, a great showman and wholly inept soldier, Custer had a screen star's love of publicity.'[57] Ethan corrects the general's misapprehension that he has been fighting Cheyenne, and is contemptuous of his hollow victory against women and children, pointing out that the Indian men were absent from the camp.

In an valuable essay on the variations between script and film, Arthur M. Eckstein argues that the omission of this scene (there's some indication it may actually have been shot)[58] is evidence that Ford considerably darkened the character of Ethan from the original conception. Had we seen Ethan opposing Custer, and implicitly supporting the Indians whom Custer has massacred, this would surely soften our view of him as an unregenerate racist.

Eckstein details a number of other differences between script and film which make Ethan 'darker and more disturbed'.[59] Principally, these are:

1. Ethan's adulterous passion for his brother's wife is emphasised more strongly in the film. The wordless scene in which the Reverend

Clayton observes Ethan and Martha's mutual affection is not scripted, though the script does make clear the nature of their relationship.

2. Towards the end of the film, Ethan enters Scar's tent after he has been killed by Marty and scalps him. This is not in the script. Eckstein rightly says that within the Western this is a highly transgressive act for a white man to perform, and shows the extent of Ethan's murderous obsession.

3. At the end of the script Ethan is holding Debbie, who is asleep, and the final image is of him riding towards the Jorgensens' house. There is no sense, as there is in the finished film, of Ethan being excluded, shut out of the house. Eckstein believes the film's ending indicates that 'Ford is punishing him for his savage racism.'[60]

On the whole this is persuasive. The Ethan of the finished film is a darker character than the Ethan of the script,[61] and a more complex one, just as the Ethan of the script (which, after all, Ford had a major role in shaping) is darker than in LeMay's original novel. However, things are not quite as clear-cut as Eckstein asserts. The issue of the scalping, for instance, is curious. In LeMay's novel Amos does scalp an Indian, the one whom the Rangers find buried under some stones while first chasing Scar: 'the Comanches believed that the spirit of a scalped warrior had to wander forever between the winds'.[62] This scene is absent in the very first version of the story, the *Saturday Evening Post* serialisation; perhaps it would have been inappropriate for a family magazine. The scalping of the entombed Indian is retained in the script, but in the film this is changed to Ethan shooting out the Indian's eyes, and the scalping displaced to the end, where it is inflicted on Scar. It's more personal; but does it make Ethan a darker character?

Furthermore, in the script Ethan is far more explicitly racist in his attitude towards Marty. After his initial remark 'fellow could mistake you for a half-breed', Ethan makes only two further references in the film to Marty's racial origins ('What does a quarter-breed Cherokee know about the old Comanche trick of sleeping with his best pony tied by his side?', and, before the incident with Futterman, when Marty says he thinks they're being followed, Ethan remarks amiably, 'That's the Indian in you'). In the script, however, Ethan cannot let the matter go. When he is shooting at the buffalo, deliberately killing them to deny the Indians food, Marty protests that 'peaceful tribes depend on the buffalo too'. Ethan sneers, 'Ain't that too bad. If you feel that sorry for your kinfolk I'm surprised you didn't take up with that squaw wife of yours.' In the film, when Look is discovered dead in the camp attacked by the army, there is unmistakable emotion in Ethan's voice when he calls Marty's attention to the body, and tenderness in the action of rubbing the snow from her hat. In the script there is no such feeling. Instead, Ethan remarks flippantly: 'Well, you're a widower now.' And in the scripted scene in the Mexican cantina, Marty (who has several more drinks than he does in the film) is dismissed by Ethan with the remark 'You breeds are all alike, two drinks an' …' Finally, we may notice that though Ethan does stand up to Custer in the scripted encounter, his contempt for the arrogant general is not because he kills Indians, which Ethan has no principled objection to, but because he fights only women and children: 'Next time you develop a village, hit it where the fightin' men are … You won't get any headlines for killing squaws.'

XVIII

Laurie completes her reading of the letter which recounts these events. Her father picks it up proprietorially and puts it in his pocket. Laurie is overcome with sorrow that Marty has no words of love in his letter: 'I don't care if he never comes back.' Mrs Jorgensen tells Charlie he must stay for supper; mindful of his opportunity he readily agrees, sidling up behind Laurie and singing a few bars of the traditional air 'Skip to my Lou'. Right now he's the fly in the buttermilk. Max Steiner's score modulates the melody into a sweetly lyrical passage for strings laid across a trade-mark Ford long-shot of Ethan and Marty outlined against the horizon at sunset. The years pass.

Steiner was the master of the lushly melodic orchestral film score, the kind of music most people associate with Hollywood in its heyday. Born in Vienna, he studied under Mahler before emigrating to Broadway to conduct musicals for Florenz Ziegfeld. He was in Hollywood almost as soon as sound itself, scoring *Cimarron* (1930), the first and until 1990 the only Western to win the Academy Award for Best Picture. Steiner worked frequently with Ford in the 30s, though his epic score for *Gone with the Wind* (1939) is probably his best known from that era, and like his great rival Dimitri Tiomkin he specialised in Westerns, memorably *Dodge City* (1939), *They Died with Their Boots On* (1941), *Pursued*, and

Distant Drums (1951). These were all Warner Bros. films, and Steiner had a long-term contract with the studio. But in the shake-out in the 50s following the divorcement of the studios from their theatre chains, such contracts were hard to find, and by the mid-50s Steiner, for all his achievements, was leading the precarious life of a freelance. Worse, his eyesight was failing.

Ford had definite ideas about what he wanted. In a memo of 28 January 1955 he wrote: 'Let's not have it written overnight by Victor Young or [Richard] Hageman.[63] This should not be done lightly but research should be done exhaustively throughout the classics of the world, from which, after all, we derive our American folk music ... find a theme that is completely haunting ... perhaps "The Yellow Rose of Texas" might be it ... "The Yellow Rose of Texas" is, after all, our theme song ... together with "Bonnie Blue Flags". Again I say, I think this is very important. ATTENTION ALL!'

The scores of Ford's Westerns place heavy reliance on traditional tunes, American or sometimes Irish folk songs. They help give them their particular flavour, root them, as does his dialogue, in the history of a people. Steiner found just the theme Ford was looking for in 'Lorena', a song written in 1857, with lyrics by the Reverend H.D.L. Webster and music by J.P. Webster, which became one of the most popular tunes of the Civil War. The lyrics tell of a lost love, blighted by a conflicting but undefined 'duty'. Though redolent of a peculiarly mid-Victorian blend of masochistic suffering, death and religiosity, they have a clear thematic connection to the frustrated passion of Ethan and Martha:

> We loved each other then, Lorena,
> More than we ever dared to tell.[64]

Steiner's masterly fusion of musical motifs drawn from different sources is first heard in the opening sequence after the credits. As the door opens outwards and we see Martha gazing into the distance, we hear 'Martha's Theme', based on 'Lorena', played by soft strings. Ethan, the former soldier of the South, rides closer and the melody changes to 'Bonnie Blue Flag', the Confederate cavalry song Ford himself had suggested, played at a reflective, lilting pace in keeping with 'Martha's Theme'. As Ethan bends to kiss Martha, there is a musical phrase from the song we have heard over the credits: 'What makes a man to wander?' Ethan's action supplies the answer. Finally, the sequence ends with a brief reprise of 'Martha's Theme' as she precedes him into the house.[65]

'Martha's Theme' will be heard in many contexts throughout the rest of the movie. As the Reverend Clayton watches Martha stroke Ethan's coat, it's played, most delicately, on a spinet, a testimony to the traditional role of the western woman as bringer of culture.[66] It's played on solo violin in a minor key as we see Ethan in close-up looking back towards the Edwards' ranch, his face full of foreboding with an intimation of the massacre; it's reprised when Debbie runs down the sand dune towards Marty near the end of the film, and perhaps most poignantly of all when at the end Ethan picks Debbie up in his arms: 'Let's go home Debbie.' 'Martha's Theme' and the main title song are the constant refrains of the film; the one reminding us of the question: 'What makes a man to wander?', the other supplying the answer: 'The story of that past, Lorena/Alas! I care not to repeat.'[67]

Steiner makes plentiful use of other traditional material: 'Skip to my Lou', the song sung to Laurie by Charlie McCorry; 'Garry Owen', the song Custer ordered his band to play at the Massacre of the Washita, used over the sequence of the cavalry in the snow; 'The Yellow Rose of Texas' at the dance before the wedding of Laurie and Charlie (Ford's own suggestion); and 'Gather at the River', the hymn tune that was practically Ford's personal anthem. It's a measure of just how cruelly Ethan tears apart the fabric of the little society of Texans that he twice interrupts this sacred song, at the ritual occasions of the funeral of Martha and her family, and at the wedding.

XIX

. . . .

The softly lyrical shot of Ethan and Marty riding at sunset dissolves to the outside of a Mexican cantina, in front of which is hitched a horse wearing a sombrero.[68] Inside we discover Mose. Ethan and Marty are both wearing wide straw hats and check shirts, Ethan's in a fetching shade of pink one suspects he wouldn't be seen dead wearing in Texas; up till now he's worn a blue or a red shirt, often with a placket-front (buttons up both sides), and suspenders (braces in England). In a memo of 10 February 1955 Ford suggested that Ethan 'may have served with Maximilian in Mexico, in which case his clothes have a Mexican touch to them. Charro spurs, a serape over the back of the saddle, a 'John' hat on his head.'[69] Then a handwritten aside: 'Mexican Saddle.' But in the event, none of this Mexican influence is evident until this late scene.

Ethan and Marty are introduced to Emilio Gabriel Fernandez y Figueroa, a dignified Mexican with a beard (played by Antonio Moreno, a veteran who had begun with D.W.Griffith and had played leads opposite Gloria Swanson and Garbo). A production memo suggests this man is a Comanchero,[70] a Mexican who traded with the Comanche, though in *The Searchers* they don't have the fearsome aspect of those Clint Eastwood meets in *The Outlaw Josey Wales*, or whom John Wayne was to meet in *The Comancheros*. But certainly we are now deep into the Hispanic hinterland, maybe even 'south of the border, down Mexico way'.

The Southwest, above and below the border, looms large in the Western, and nowhere more so than in Ford's films. Elsewhere I've remarked on the Hispanic references in *Stagecoach* and *My Darling Clementine*, where whole sections of dialogue are in Spanish.[71] Other Ford Westerns have a strongly Hispanic flavour. One of the leading roles in *3 Godfathers* is played by the Mexican star Pedro Armendariz, who also has a significant role in *Fort Apache* and in *The Fugitive*, Ford's version of *The Power and the Glory*, Graham Greene's novel about a Mexican priest. Ford's later Western, *Two Rode Together*, centres on the rescue from Indians of a Mexican woman (played by Linda Cristal, an Argentinian who originally made her name in Mexican cinema).

The bearded man is dressed in Mexican finery: red embroidered velvet jacket, tight-fitting trousers, sombrero, jingling silver spurs. As he calls for a better quality tequila, a woman appears and does a few twirls to the rhythm of her castanets. Ethan and the Mexican converse in Spanish; in fact much of the scene is conducted in Spanish (at this point the Spanish-language version of the film simply reproduces the dialogue of the original version – though revoiced.). While Ethan and Figueroa talk, Marty sits down to Mexican food, beans and tortillas. He too can get by in Spanish ('mas frijoles'); though only up to a point. Ethan announces he's off to meet Cicatriz. 'Never heard of him,' Marty says. 'Cicatriz is Mexican for Scar,' Ethan says, punctuating his remark by throwing Marty's tequila on the fire, where it explodes. It's a gesture previously encountered in *Stagecoach*, where Doc Boone throws his whiskey in the fire.

The Hispanic flavour of the scene is perhaps no more than the manipulation of recognisable, conventional signs: the tequila, the tortillas, the sombreros, the castanets, the 'loose' woman who tries to capture Marty's interest (in the script she succeeds; in the film he's more interested in the food). But it gives us a sense of just how far Ethan and Marty have travelled, that they are now outside their home territory, are truly Texicans 'way out on a limb'.

Figueroa takes them to Scar's camp, located in some of the most magical scenery of any American picture, on some sand dunes by a tall thin rock called, appropriately, Totem Pole, in the south-east corner of Monument Valley (the same site is used for the Cheyenne camp in *Cheyenne Autumn*).[72] After the ritual exchange of hostilities ('Scar, huh? Plain to see how you got your name') they enter Scar's tent. There at last Ethan and Marty catch sight of what they have been searching for all these years.

Figueroa gestures towards a group of four women sitting at the back of the tepee, Scar's wives. Two of his sons are dead, he says, killed by whites. For each one, he has taken many white scalps. The endless cycle of tit-for-tat revenge will culminate in Ethan's taking of Scar's own scalp. Scar orders one of his wives to show the white men his trophies. A pole with hair dangling from it is thrust before them, and they look up at the woman holding it. Natalie Wood is dressed in a pinkish-brown velvet blouse and purple skirt, with silver conch belt, braided hair and Indian ornaments around her neck.[73] But unmistakably she is a white woman.

Natalie Wood turned eighteen while the picture was being shot. But she was already a seasoned performer, a child star who had made a successful transition to adult roles the year before, playing opposite James Dean in *Rebel Without a Cause*.[74] For someone who has spent years as a Comanche captive, she looks remarkably well-groomed. But the film is not really interested in the details of Debbie's life with the Indians. We don't look to the Western for ethnography. From time to time movies have attempted some insights into Native American culture; *Broken Arrow*, perhaps, or *Apache*, or more recently *Dances with Wolves*. Mick Gidley records in his book on Edward S. Curtis, the foremost photographer of Indians, that in the earliest days of the Western movie there were calls in the film trade press for more accurate and detailed representations of Indian life. *Moving Picture World* wrote in 1911:

While we still have the real Indians with us, why cannot thoroughly representative films be produced, making them at once illustrative and historic recorders of this noble race of people, with their splendid physique and physical powers. ... It is to be hoped that some of our Western manufacturers will yet produce a series of REAL Indian life ...[75]

But the call fell on deaf ears. Hollywood wanted stories, characters, action, not education.

As a character Debbie barely exists; she is merely the object of the search. And despite her protestations in the next scene that she has all but forgotten her past, that the Comanche are her people now, such is her beauty that anyone would surely wish to rescue her. Anyone except Ethan, that is. Debbie appears over the top of a sand dune as Ethan and Marty discuss their next move. As she runs down the slope we hear 'Lorena' once more on the soundtrack. But Ethan has stopped his ears against the siren call of kith and kin. As Debbie begs Marty and Ethan to leave, Ethan draws his gun to kill her. When Marty steps in front of her, a tragic ending to the tale threatens. It is prevented by a Comanche arrow, which takes Ethan in the shoulder. He and Marty ride off, the Comanche in hot pursuit. No sooner have they found Debbie than they have lost her again.

When Ethan and Marty find cover in a cave, the Indians mass for attack (another futile frontal assault). Scar dons his war bonnet, as he had done in the battle at the river, and he and two companions ride full tilt towards a camera set in a pit in the ground, passing overhead, a favourite shot of Ford's from the silent days. When Scar's horse is shot from under him, the Indians abandon their attack. Holed up in the cave, severely wounded, Ethan writes his will. He gives it to Marty to read, which he does, as usual stumbling over the words. It states that Ethan, being 'without any blood kin', is leaving his property to Marty. When Marty protests that Debbie is his kin, Ethan replies that she isn't any more, since 'she's been living with a buck'. Ethan's is a particularly virulent form of racism. The taint of association with Indians is so great that it overcomes the ties of blood between him and his niece. Only death, he thinks, can purge her of such contamination. Marty, by contrast, the half-breed who has no blood ties, is the one who redeems her.

XX
. . . .

When Ethan and Marty draw up once more outside the Jorgensens', we are in the middle of a dance. In Ford's films dances are an affirmation of the community, that sense of social belonging which is at the heart of his films, perhaps most movingly rendered in the 'dag-blasted good dance' at the half-built church of Tombstone in *My Darling Clementine*.[76] The party is to celebrate the wedding of Laurie and Charlie, but when, after an absence that may be months or years, Ethan and Marty arrive outside the Jorgensens' house, Marty wonders if perhaps the party is for them. (Why? Surely no one knows they are coming.) Ethan's response is exactly the same as his reply in the previous scene to Marty's bitter outburst against his disowning of Debbie, 'I hope you die': 'That'll be the day.' It's the third time he uses the catch-phrase. (Earlier, in objecting to Ethan's assertion that Lucy and Debbie may be dead, Brad offered to fight Ethan. 'That'll be the day,' says Ethan dismissively.) The first time the phrase asserts his superior strength, the second his indomitable will, and the third, humorously, his status as outsider.[77]

While Ethan goes to investigate, Marty sees Laurie in her wedding dress. 'Looks like you two'll have a lot to talk about,' says Ethan, as usual enjoying Marty's discomfort. Laurie complains to Marty that he only ever wrote one letter, and even that didn't say he loved her. Marty offers the traditional male defence down the ages: 'But I always loved you. I thought you knew that without me having to say it.' Laurie breaks down and cries. 'It isn't fair.' Marty can fight Comanche but he can't fight tears. 'I wish you wouldn't cry, Laurie.' In a typically Fordian mix of comedy and pathos, Laurie sobs, 'Who's crying?' (another remark not in the script). As they embrace, Charlie makes an appearance, uncomfortable in brown derby hat and white gloves. In the script he says: 'I'll thank ya to leave the room, Laurie.' But, wishing to make the most of Charlie's drollness, Ford has him remark, his stiff formality contrasting with his hick accent: 'I'll thank you to unhand my fiancée.' After an initial scuffle, in which Marty once more falls back over the settle ('Marty, you done it again,' cries Laurie) they agree to fight outside. In an elaborate display of etiquette, Marty helps Charlie off with his coat and hat, while Charlie conducts the

Frederic Remington, *A Beautiful Fight Ensued* (c. 1899)

ritual ('spit over that piece of firewood'). Marty's method of fighting is unorthodox – he bites Charlie's leg, then his hand, but the Reverend Clayton arrives to regulate the contest: 'No biting or gouging and no kicking either.'

Ford loved a comic fight. In the cavalry trilogy Victor McLaglen gave an unsurpassed exhibition of the art of farcical fisticuffs. It's a long-standing tradition in the Western. Frederic Remington, whose paintings did so much to codify the stock situations of the Western narrative, did a picture entitled *A Beautiful Fight Ensued*, in which a group of cavalry soldiers set about each other in a bar. In the 1942 Western *The Spoilers* there's an epic fight between John Wayne and Randolph Scott, and in *North to Alaska* (1960) Wayne and Stewart Granger take apart the town of Nome piece by piece. This time Wayne is not involved, and the fight between Marty and Charlie is a small-scale affair, but it provides good entertainment for all, not least the ladies.

XXI

. . . .

After the fight is over, Clayton tells Ethan and Marty they must accompany him to Austin, the state capital, where charges have been laid against them for the murder of Futterman. But this business is fated never to be resolved, since they are interrupted by a young cavalry lieutenant, played by Pat Wayne, John Wayne's son. Wayne Sr and Ward Bond enjoy themselves immensely in this scene, unsettling the youngster by constantly interrupting, though in a good spirit: 'Just funning, son.' The soldiers have discovered Mose, who has been captured by Scar but has escaped. Mose's search for the security of a rocking chair by the fire has been an echo of Ethan's own wandering; indeed, Ethan sits in the rocking chair when he first arrives at the Edwards' ranch, and later at the Jorgensens'. Mose is in a long tradition of Fordian oddities, drunks and simpletons who are welcomed with Christian charity into the inner circle, and who had often been acted by Ford's older brother Francis (who died in 1953). Mose's frequent jokes ('That which we are about to receive, we thank thee, oh Lord,' he intones as the Indians attack) make him a sort of fool to Ethan's Lear. In the last scene, Mose is rewarded for his fidelity, rocking contentedly on the Jorgensens' porch.

Mose provides the information they need to find Scar. The Rangers under Clayton assemble near the Comanche camp, where Ethan makes it clear he is calculating on Debbie being murdered the moment they attack. Marty insists he be allowed to get Debbie out first. Ethan makes a last effort to dissuade him by revealing that it was his mother's scalp on the pole in Scar's camp, but Marty is motivated not by revenge but by his desire to reconstitute his adopted family – the very thing which Ethan professes.

Clayton, who after all is in command, overrules Ethan and allows Marty to precede them into the Comanche camp. Marty is dropped over a ledge (a feature in Monument Valley known as John Ford's Point). Things now move rapidly towards a conclusion. In the Comanche camp Scar is disturbed by a noise. Will Marty be discovered? Then we cut back to the Rangers. Once more Ford alternates comedy and high drama. The young lieutenant turns up again, to be summarily dismissed by Clayton: 'Good work, son, good work. Good bye.' On protest he's allowed to stay, then nearly decapitates Clayton when he draws his sabre, an action which sets up further comedy for the penultimate scene. The Rangers advance on foot, Clayton and the lieutenant, Ethan, Charlie and another Ranger (Chuck Roberson), then Nesby and another. Clayton gives the order: 'Mount.' The lieutenant is slow to respond. 'M-O-N-T-E, mount!' Clayton hollers. The scene ends with Ethan riding forward, closer to the camera, staring into the distance. As so often, his face focuses our thoughts.

Cut again back to the Comanche camp. We see what Ethan could only imagine. Marty finds Scar's tent. Inside, he tells Debbie he's come to take her away. 'Yes, Marty,' she whispers. Why she should have changed her mind since the last encounter is simply not explained. But Scar has been alerted. We see him at the opening of the tent, from the waist down only. He brings his rifle forward, but Marty is quicker, turning and firing three shots from his Colt, their flashes lighting up the screen. Cut to the Rangers. 'Brethren, leave us go amongst them,' says Clayton, combining his role of captain with that of biblical patriarch. In a fast tracking shot the Rangers charge through the Comanche camp, Ethan at their head. Knocking over a woman carrying a baby, he rides his horse into Scar's tent. Seizing the lifeless body of the chief, he draws his bowie knife. The Rangers wheel for another charge. But though there's plenty of gunfire, with women and children scattering, not one Indian is seen to be killed in the attack. Instead, the Rangers run off the horses, thereby rendering the Comanche impotent.

Scar is the only casualty; it's personal. Ethan emerges from the tent, the scalp clearly visible in his hand. There is a large close-up, Ethan's face expressing – what? Not exactly hatred or determination; it's more of a perplexed look as he gazes off screen. Cut to the fleeing Debbie, who has somehow become detached from Marty in the confusion. Ethan rides after her, brushing aside Marty's attempt to stop him. Debbie runs down a slope with Ethan in pursuit. There's a cut to a shot from within a cave, the sides of the screen masked by dark rock, as at the centre we watch Ethan corner the defenceless girl.

There's no narrative motivation for this shot. No one is in the cave looking out, nor does anyone enter it. But it has a stylistic connection to others in the film, and Ford uses such a composition on no fewer than eight other occasions. It's worth listing them. The first shot of the film is from inside the Edwards' house, looking out. Then we see Marty arrive at the house, looking out at him from inside. We also have a similar shot of Brad and Lucy kissing. When Ethan arrives back after the Indian attack, there's a shot of him from inside the store-house, where Martha's mutilated body lies. Later, when Ethan and Marty arrive back at the Jorgensens' we see them from inside the house. Then at the Indian camp which has been attacked by the cavalry there's a shot from within a tepee, as Ethan enters to discover the body of Look. When Ethan and Marty are chased by Scar's men, they go towards a cave and a shot frames them from within. And there's the final shot of the film, of which more shortly.

What have all these shots got in common, besides their striking framing? The effect is not unlike the iris shot so beloved of early silent directors such as D.W.Griffith, isolating a figure in the frame. But it's more than that. In each case the camera is positioned in a place of refuge, a dark, womb-like space which offers a secure view to the world outside. Or ought to; for in two of these shots we are placed within a space that has been sacrilegiously defiled, in which the body of a dead woman lies. At the pivotal moment in the film, as Ethan runs down Debbie in order to kill her, and she strives to reach the security of the cave, it looks as though for a third time a place of safety will become a woman's tomb.

But, in a complete and unexpected reversal, instead of murdering her, Ethan stoops, picks up Debbie and raises her aloft, in an exact repeat of his gesture all those years ago when he greeted her as a little girl at the Edwards' ranch. As he cradles her in his arms, the soundtrack reprises 'Martha's Theme'. 'Let's go home, Debbie,' says Ethan; surely the most moving yet bitterly ironic words in Ford.[78]

All Ford's films are about home: finding it, building it, losing it. No scene is more affecting than that in *The Grapes of Wrath*, when the Joad family depart from the little shack they call home, cast adrift into a rootless world. Ethan would not be the last role Wayne played for Ford in which he ends up homeless; in *The Man Who Shot Liberty Valance*, having lost the love of his life he burns down the house he was building for her.

Before the final scene there's one more instalment of comedy. Clayton, bent over, his trousers about his knees, yells in pain as some astringent is poured on his backside. The censor from the Production Code Office was nervous about this. 'The handling of the scene in which Clayton's wound is being treated will require great restraint in order to avoid vulgarity.' As usual, the censor missed the point. Without the vulgarity there would be no humour.[79]

Eight shots complete the film. We dissolve to the porch of the Jorgensen house, on which sits Mose, rocking in his chair. Mrs and Mr Jorgensen come out to stand on the porch, looking out. Cut to a shot across some water, a horse in the foreground, in the background five riders approaching. Cut back to the porch: Laurie comes out and stands centre frame for a moment, then runs forward. Cut to a shot of Laurie running away from the camera towards the line of riders. At the head is Ethan, with Debbie on his saddle in front of him. Behind is Marty, then

Wayne's homage to
Harry Carey

Clayton and the others. Laurie holds on to Marty's saddle. Cut to Mrs and
Mr Jorgensen, he gesturing with his pipe as she covers her head with her
apron, overcome with tears. Cut to a shot of Ethan dismounting and
lifting Debbie down. As he does so we hear The Sons of the Pioneers:

> A man will search his heart and soul
> Go searching way out there
> His peace of mind he knows he'll find
> But where, oh Lord, Lord where?

A close-up of Mose, who puts his hat on. And now the last shot, carefully
composed. Looking from the dark interior of the house we see Ethan
approach, carrying Debbie. He sets her down in front of the Jorgensens,
who take her inside. Ethan looks to join them, but as he moves forward,
Marty and Laurie come from behind him. He moves aside to let them pass
into the house. Then he stands on the porch, feet astride. His left hand
comes across his body to hold his right arm at the elbow. He turns and
walks straight out into the desert. The door closes on him.

In a television interview with Kevin Brownlow,[80] Wayne explained
that he performed the arm gesture as a homage to Harry Carey, the star of
Ford's early Westerns, whose wife and son appear in the film. Garry
Wills rightly takes Tag Gallagher to task for trying to offer plausible
narrative explanations for Ethan's turning away, such as 'new duties
call'.[81] No such explanations are needed; the act is deeply satisfying at a
symbolic level. Ethan may have relented from his intention to murder
Debbie, but he is a man doomed to wander. There is no place for him
within the home, for him no 'peace of mind'. Ride away.[82]

XXII

Once the film was completed, Warners got behind it with enthusiasm. A new edition of Alan LeMay's novel was rushed out, and Tex Ritter recorded the theme song for Capitol Records. 'He had to find her, he had to find her' was the strap line for the posters, though some of the suggestions in the press book for publicity stunts hardly matched the grandeur of the film ('Dress men in Western outfits. Provide with outsize divining-rods or mine detectors and get them to parade town pretending to search for something under the pavement. ...') The film was warmly received by the critics. Bosley Crowther in the *New York Times* said it had 'the toughness of leather and the sting of a whip', taking issue only with those scenes shot in the 'obviously synthetic surroundings of the studio stage'. The *Los Angeles Times* was equally appreciative, both of the film's suspense and its humour, while the *Los Angeles Examiner* was quite carried away:

> The grandeur, the beauty, the sweep and the tragic horror of the newest John Wayne–John Ford classic of the old West, *The Searchers*, cannot, with justice, be detailed by mere words. Its scope is simply tremendous. Its motivation spine chillingly grim. Its setting the most starkly beautiful ever seen in a Western film. The majestic rock formations of Monument Valley, the panoramas of buttes and mesas, the desert of New Mexico, in Technicolor and Vista Vision [sic], are beyond description.[83]

British critics agreed. Leonard Mosley in the *Daily Express* called it 'the best Western I have seen in ten years'. Alan Brien in the *Evening Standard* spoke of 'breathtaking grandeur' and Dilys Powell in the *Sunday Times* called it 'a Western of the first rank ... I could not rest until I had seen it again, and all through'.[84]

The trade press had already pronounced the film a success, though not without some misgivings. *Variety* called it an 'exciting Western in the grand scale' and 'a contender for the big money stakes'.[85] But it wondered if the film was a trifle too long, found Wayne's character perplexing and called the comedy 'labored'. *Motion Picture Herald* had no such reservations, calling the film 'one of the greatest of the great pictures of the American West'.[86] The reviewer of *Hollywood Reporter* concurred: 'undoubtedly one of the greatest Westerns ever made. For sheer scope, guts, and beauty I can think of no picture of the Indian Wars of the Southwest to compare with it.'[87] The reviewer singled out the 'hilarious' fight between Marty and Charlie, and observed that female interest in the film is sustained by having Laurie react to Marty's letter. Ford's comedy was clearly a matter of taste, since the *Film Daily* reviewer found it 'jarring', though in general it was enthusiastic.[88]

The film performed creditably at the box office, grossing $5,413,601.13 by 30 November 1957. (Of this $1,147,545.95 came from foreign receipts.)[89] Box-office figures are notoriously unreliable, but in Joel Finler and David Pirie's list of all-time Western champs, in which figures are adjusted for inflation, *The Searchers* comes seventeenth in the table, an excellent result.[90]

XXIII

In the contemporary chorus of praise, one voice stood out in dissent. In *Sight and Sound* Lindsay Anderson, long a champion of Ford, could find little to say in favour. He objected that there was too much story (Ford's most successful films rely on mood, not narrative, he asserted). Worse, Ethan is 'an unmistakable neurotic', and Wayne's performance 'lacks either complexity or consistency'. In Anderson's opinion the comedy which follows the moments of high drama 'completely destroys any tension in the situation or characters'. (Would he have said the same about the porter scene in *Macbeth*?) Returning to the film in his book *About John Ford* in 1981, Anderson was not inclined to revise his view that it was 'not among John Ford's masterpieces'.[91]

It is nearly half a century since *The Searchers* appeared. Every year since has rendered Anderson's view of the film even more eccentric than when it was published, as the consensus has built that this is one of the great masterpieces of American cinema. True, there have since been other dissenting voices. Despite her influence with Paul Schrader, Martin Scorsese and other American film-makers of their generation, Pauline Kael never seems to have understood their fascination with *The Searchers*, calling it 'peculiarly formal and stilted ... You can read a lot into it, but it isn't very enjoyable. The lines are often awkward, and the line readings worse, and the film is often static': one of Kael's more astonishing misjudgements.[92] David Thomson, though he allows *The Searchers* to be 'a riveting, tragic, and complex experience', has called Ford 'trite, callow and evasive', his Westerns 'fraudulent'.[93] But this is very much a minority view. In the 1972 *Sight and Sound* worldwide poll of critics' favourite films, *The Searchers* was in seventeenth place. By 1982 it had risen to ninth, and in 1992 to fifth; could it go even higher in 2002?[94]

The critical literature on the film continues to grow, as the bibliography indicates. More surprising, perhaps, is the effect the film has had on film-makers, especially Americans. In a 1979 article, Stuart Byron cited eleven films which show evidence of influence. Paul Schrader's *Hardcore* recounts the obsessive search of a father for a daughter who has fallen into an alien culture, in this case the world of pornography. Schrader admits *The Searchers* as a source, and also allows that *Taxi Driver*, which he scripted for Scorsese, has a strikingly similar narrative structure. Scorsese's *Mean Streets* actually contains a clip of *The Searchers*, and his early feature *Who's That Knocking at My Door?* has an extended passage of dialogue in which Harvey Keitel cross-questions a girl about *The Searchers*. John Milius has something of an obsession with the film, naming his son Ethan and constantly working references into his work. *Dillinger* has an echo of the first scene of *The Searchers*, *Big Wednesday* refers to the last scene, and in *The Wind and the Lion* a soldier plays part of the score.[95] In 1991 the National Film Theatre in London presented a season of films influenced by *The Searchers* or related by theme. In addition to the above titles it included: *Ulzana's Raid*; *Major Dundee*; *Rolling Thunder*; *Year of the Dragon*; *Dog Soldiers*; *Paris, Texas*; *The Emerald Forest*; *Dances with Wolves*; and Ford's own *Two Rode Together*. Yet even this can hardly be an exhaustive list.[96]

XXIV

. . . .

At the dawn of the second century of cinema *The Searchers* stands, by general assent, as a monument no less conspicuous than the towers of stone which dominate its landscapes. The strength yet delicacy of its *mise en scène*, the splendour of its vistas, the true timbre of its emotions, make it a touchstone of American cinema. *The Searchers* is one of those films by which Hollywood may be measured. But the judgement of its worth cannot only be in terms of its beauty. The film has claims not only upon our eyes or feelings, but upon our minds. Ford set out, according to his lights, to make a film about the perennial American problem of race. His desire to make a statement is clear: 'The audience likes to see Indians get killed. They don't consider them as human beings – with a great culture of their own – quite different from ours.'[97] Being Ford, he both shows Ethan for what he is, a murderous racist, and yet draws out our pity for him. To some, perhaps, this will seem like equivocation. But in my view it's the greatness of the film. The contradictions of Ethan's character, his compelling strength matched only by his repellent bigotry, cannot be easily resolved, forcing us to a more painful awareness than the pieties of more obviously liberal films.[98] Only once, in the coarse comedy of the 'marriage' to Look, does Ford's touch falter. Otherwise, his gaze is steady but compassionate. At the end, just at the moment of truth when Ethan has found love in his heart and not hate, Ford does not shirk the stern judgement. The door closes on him and shuts him out from human warmth and companionship. Yet who as the screen goes black does not feel Ethan's tragedy?

NOTES

· ·

1 Ford was to change his mind about how the film should open, but he settled on Ethan's costume at an early stage, writing in a memo of 28 January 1955: 'This man [...] is dressed in a ragged, caped overcoat of Confederate gray. On his sleeve, three ragged red sergeant's chevrons. A plain black hat and Yankee officer's cavalry britches with yellow stripe ... much worn. His shirt should be a Johnny Reb butternut.' (James Nottage informs me that during the Civil War the South had a shortage of dye stuff and had to colour cloth with plant material, including nuts. Butternut was one of the colours so produced. In the film it's Ethan's grey overcoat that is referred to as a Johnny Reb, not his shirt.)

2 There's an odd continuity lapse in the opening scene. A Navajo blanket is seen first beside Debbie, in a later shot it moves to the hitching post in front of house, then later it's gone altogether. Peter Lehman tries to read this thematically, in his essay, '"There's no way of knowing" – Analysis of *The Searchers*' in William Luhr and Peter Lehman, *Authorship and Narrative in the Cinema* (New York: G. P. Putnam's Sons, 1977), p. 121.

3 These scenes are not the opening Ford first thought of. In a memo of 28 January 1955 he writes: 'The screen opens up on a prairie scene and slowly into the picture comes the biggest steer, with the biggest spread of horns we can get. After sufficient footage the credits appear. Through the credits, the Longhorns drift horizontally across the screen. After the finish of the credits we go to the typical, trail herd. Into this scene rides ... he doesn't trot, gallop or canter, he just walks his horse to the "point" ... to the cowpunch in the lead and begins dialogue.' The original novel by Alan LeMay is different again, beginning with the Edwards' ranch at dusk as the Indians gather unseen outside and the family prepares for attack.

4 Questioned by Peter Bogdanovich, Ford said Ethan 'probably went over into Mexico, became a bandit, probably fought for Juarez or Maximilian, because of the medal'. Peter Bogdanovich, *John Ford* (London: Studio Vista, 1967), pp. 92–3.

5 Speaking to Bogdanovich, Ford thought it 'pretty obvious' (p. 93). But in a memo of 15 February 1955 he wanted to point it up a bit more: 'The only time he betrays his feeling for her is seen after his arrival at his brother's house. He and Martha are alone. Amos [renamed Ethan] takes her hand, caresses it, examines it and says tenderly, somewhat awkwardly, "You work hard, don't you, Martha?" She looks at him with a shyness of a mature woman afraid to exhibit the emotions she can barely control. She says nothing.' This scene is not in the film.

6 Quoted in Lindsay Anderson, *About John Ford* (London: Plexus, 1981), p. 244.

7 In demanding his military title, is Clayton mindful of the remark of his near namesake, Dr Johnson: 'Every man thinks meanly of himself for not having been a soldier'?

8 The complete lyrics are:

> The horizon's like a woman
> With her arms flung open wide
> And a man that's trying to fill his heart
> Ain't got no place to hide.
>
> What makes a man to wander
> What makes a man to roam?
> What makes a man leave bed and board
> And turn his back on home?
>
> Now a man will search for fortune
> Of silver and of gold
> The silver he finds in his hair
> While a weary heart grows old.
>
> Some men search for injuns
> Or hump-backed buffalo
> And even when they found them
> They move on lonesome slow.
>
> The rustling of the dry brown leaves
> Along the frosty ground
> Whispers soft of autumn time
> But a wanderer fears that sound.
>
> The snow is deep and oh so white
> The winds they howl and mourn
> Fire cooks a man his meat
> But his lonely heart won't warm.

A man will search his heart and soul
Go searching way out there
His peace of mind he knows he'll find
But where, oh Lord, Lord where?

Me I go on searching
For where there ain't no hate
For a tender love I'm dreaming of
A'fore it gets too late.

Ride away, ride away, ride away.

9 Jane Tompkins, *West of Everything: The Inner Life of Westerns* (New York: Oxford University Press, 1992), pp. 42f.

10 One of the Comanche leaders in this conflict was Quanah Parker, the son of Cynthia Ann Parker, a white woman captured by the Comanche who became the wife of the chief Peta Nocona; according to John Milius, speaking in a documentary about the making of *The Searchers* included in the laser-disk version of the film, this forms the basis of Alan LeMay's original story on which *The Searchers* is based. Milius gives no evidence for this assertion. (Quanah Parker also appears as a character in John Ford's *Two Rode Together*, where he is played by the same Henry Brandon who plays Scar in *The Searchers*.)

11 Ford's use of Western locations has been extensively researched by Carlo Gaberscek in *Il West di John Ford* (Udine: Arti Grafiche Friulane, 1994).

12 Edward Buscombe, 'Inventing Monument Valley: Nineteenth-Century Landscape Photography and the Western Film', in Patrice Petro (ed.), *Fugitive Images: From Photography to Video* (Bloomington: Indiana University Press, 1995).

13 David W. Teague, *The Southwest in American Literature and Art: The Rise of a Desert Aesthetic* (Tucson: University of Arizona Press, 1997), p. 3.

14 Frederick Jackson Turner, *The Frontier in American History* (New York: Holt, Rinehart Winston, 1962).

15 Quoted in Donald J. Hagerty, *Desert Dreams: The Art and Life of Maynard Dixon* (Layton, Utah: Peregrine Smith Books, 1993), p. 153.

16 Stephen J. Pyne, *How the Canyon Became Grand: A Short History* (New York: Penguin, 1999), p. 110.

17 Ibid., p. 51.

18 Ibid, pp. 118f.

19 See the entry in *Film Dope*, no. 24, March 1982.

20 Was Harry Carey Jr originally cast as Charlie? In a memo of 27 January 1955 Ford speaks of the fight at the dance being between Marty and 'Dobie', the nickname of Harry Carey Jr. However, in his memoirs, *Company of Heroes: My Life as an Actor in the John Ford Stock Company* (Lanham, Maryland: Madison Books, 1996), Carey makes no mention of this.

21 See Edward Buscombe (ed.), *The BFI Companion to the Western* (London: André Deutsch/BFI Publishing, 1988), p. 79.

22 One example was the case of Eunice Williams; see John Demos, *The Unredeemed Captive: A Family Story from Early America* (London: Papermac, 1996).

23 Kathryn Zabelle Derounian-Stodola, *Women's Indian Captivity Narratives* (New York: Penguin, 1998), p. xvii.

24 Ethan never says what kind of a medal it is. The crown at the top might suggest an origin in the Mexican empire of Maximilian.

25 It's noticeable that the Indian in the grave is breathing; Ford could be careless of such details.

26 It is in his analysis of the Leatherstocking novels that D.H.Lawrence makes his oft-quoted statement, 'The essential American soul is hard, isolate, stoic, and a killer. It has never yet melted. ... Deerslayer [is] a man who turns his back on white society. A man who keeps his moral integrity hard and intact. An isolate, almost selfless, stoic, enduring man, who lives by death, by killing, but who is pure white.' D.H.Lawrence, *Selected Literary Criticism* (London: Mercury Books, 1956), p. 329. As a description of Ethan this has a chilling accuracy, except that at the very last he does melt, as he picks Debbie up in his arms.

27 Carey, *Company of Heroes* p. 167.

28 Ibid., p. 27.

29 Quoted in Todd McCarthy, *Howard Hawks, The Grey Fox of Hollywood* (New York: Grove Press, 1997), p. 445.

30 On the DVD version of the film you can hear Wayne dubbed into both French and Spanish. Perhaps only then do you realise just how much his voice brings to the film.

31 Peter Wollen, *Signs and Meaning in the Cinema* (London: Secker & Warburg, 1972), p. 96.

32 Chief Big Tree, given speaking parts in *Drums Along the Mohawk* and *She Wore a Yellow Ribbon*, was an exception.

33 Jacquelyn Kilpatrick suggests that Ethan might in fact have killed Lucy himself, as he later tries to kill Debbie. See *Celluloid Indians: Native Americans and Film* (Lincoln: University of Nebraska Press, 1999), p. 61.

34 'The architectural style of Jorgensen's house is the simplified Gothic style that was recommended to Christians in the middle of the nineteenth century as a witness to their religious faith.' Richard Hutson, 'Sermons in Stone: Monument Valley in *The Searchers*' in Leonard Engel (ed.), *The Big Empty: Essays on Western Landscapes as Narrative* (Albuquerque: University of New Mexico Press, 1994), p. 204.

35 J. Mauduy and G. Henriet, *Géographies du Western* (Paris: Nathan, 1989), p. 23.

36 In a memo of 10 February 1955 it had been chickens, not pigs.

37 The letter is among Ford's correspondence in the Lilly Library.

38 Dan Ford says Whitney was 'heir to the Minnesota Mining and Manufacturing fortune'. Dan Ford, *Pappy: The Life of John Ford* (New York: Da Capo, 1998), p. 270.

39 C.V. Whitney, *High Peaks* (Lexington: University Press of Kentucky, 1977), p. 91.

40 At the risk of self-plagiarism, I'd like to quote a footnote to an article from 1984:

> For those with a taste for the by-ways of historical coincidence, Ford's *The Searchers* provides a labyrinthine example of the interconnections between the 'real' West and the construction of its representations. The film was produced by Cornelius Vanderbilt Whitney, a distant descendant of the Eli Whitney who invented the system of mass producing guns through the use of interchangeable parts and so provided cheap reliable weaponry for the conquest of the West. C. V. Whitney was also a cousin [actually, the son] of the Gertrude Vanderbilt Whitney who founded the Whitney Gallery of Western Art in Cody, Wyoming, where some of [Frederic] Remington's pictures are preserved. McBride and Wilmington in their book on Ford speculate that the name of the hero of *The Searchers*, Ethan Edwards, is an amalgamation of Ethan Allen, the Revolutionary hero [and now the name of a chain of American furniture stores], and Jonathan Edwards, the preacher. They might have added that Eli Whitney was in fact married to Jonathan Edwards's granddaughter. (Edward Buscombe, 'Painting the Legend: Frederic Remington and the Western', *Cinema Journal*, 23/4, Summer 1984.)

41 See Ford, *Pappy*, p. 270.

42 Quoted in Anderson, *About John Ford* p. 242.

43 Garry Wills, *John Wayne: The Politics of Celebrity* (London: Faber and Faber, 1997), p. 252. In the list of the most popular boys' names in the UK for 1999 Ethan stood at no. 47, up seven places from the previous year. *Guardian*, 5 January 1999.

44 Alan LeMay, *The Searchers* (London: Corgi, 1963), p. 210.

45 A letter from Geoffrey M. Shurlock at the Production Code Office (20 June 1955) objected: 'The sequence of Martin taking a bath with Laurie in the room is, we feel, unacceptable and some other business should be substituted in its place.' The letter is in the Margaret Herrick Library, Academy of Motion Picture Arts and Sciences.

46 Dudley Nichols, who wrote many of Ford's films, told Lindsay Anderson, 'I cannot recall one of his films in which the man–woman relationship came off with any feeling or profundity'; a harsh judgement, surely. Quoted in Anderson, *About John Ford*, p. 241.

47 Under the apron she's wearing a check shirt and jeans, the uniform of 50s American suburbia. Western costume often has more to do with the time when the film was made than with historical authenticity. No farmer's daughter in Texas in 1868 would have worn trousers, whatever the occasion.

48 Ford's most daring use of comedy is in the Wyatt Earp sequence in the otherwise tragic *Cheyenne Autumn*.

49 See Donald Spoto, *The Dark Side of Genius: The Life of Alfred Hitchcock* (London: Plexus, 1994), pp. 375f.

50 In the Ford papers at the Lilly Library, a note in box 8, file 22 says that Ford will be paid $175,000 for twenty-six weeks' work, plus 10% of net profits. The distribution agreement, a copy of which is in the Warner Bros. Archives at the Doheny Library, University of Southern California, calls for C.V. Whitney Pictures to deliver to Warners 'a final budget indicating photoplay's anticipated total negative cost of production'. I have been unable to locate such a budget.

51 Tag Gallagher, *John Ford: The Man and His Films* (Berkeley: University of California Press, 1986), p. 326.

52 Carey, *Company of Heroes*, p. 167.

53 Jane Tompkins, determined to hammer home her indictment of the Western as repressive of the female, ignores this speech in her account of the film:

> In this story [*The Searchers*], as in many Westerns, women are the motive for male activity (it's women who are being avenged, it's a woman the men are trying to rescue) at the same time as what women stand for – love and forgiveness in place of vengeance – is precisely what the activity denies. Time after time, the Western hero commits murder, usually multiple murders, in the name of making his town/ranch/ mining claim safe for women and children. But the discourse of love and peace which women articulate is never listened to … (Tompkins, *West of Everything*, p. 41.)

Clearly Tompkins did not listen to Laurie's speech, nor to any of Marty's counter-arguments.

54 Richard Maltby argues, following Brian Henderson, that Ethan's racism in respect of

Marty is inconsistent. But being irrational, its inconsistency is hardly surprising. See Richard Maltby, 'John Ford and the Indians; or, Tom Doniphon's History Lesson' in Mick Gidley (ed.), *Representing Others: White Views of Indigenous Peoples* (Exeter: University of Exeter Press, 1992), p. 131.

55 Peter Lehman has no doubt of how we are meant to respond, accusing Ford in this scene of behaving 'like a schoolboy' in his 'vicious and brutal treatment of Look'. Peter Lehman, 'Texas 1868/America 1956: *The Searchers*' in Lehman (ed.), *Close Viewings* (Tallahassee: Florida State University Press, 1990).

56 There are similar scenes with journalists, meta-discourses if you will, in *Fort Apache* and *The Man Who Shot Liberty Valance*.

57 The memo of 15 February specifically identifies the massacre of Indians which Ethan and Marty discover as the Washita Massacre, carried out by Custer's troops on a sleeping Cheyenne camp at dawn on 27 November 1868.

58 Paul Hutton reproduces a still from *The Searchers* of John Wayne with Peter Ortiz playing Custer, in his essay '"Correct in Every Detail": General Custer in Hollywood', *Montana, The Magazine of Western History*, 41/1, Winter 1991, p. 44.

59 Arthur M. Eckstein, 'John Ford's *The Searchers* (1956) from Novel to Screenplay to Screen', *Cinema Journal*, 38/1, Fall 1998, p. 4.

60 Ibid., p. 15.

61 Though Garry Wills (*John Wayne*, p. 254) says Ford made Ethan 'more sympathetic' than the novel.

62 LeMay, *The Searchers*, p. 29.

63 Victor Young wrote the music for *Rio Grande*, *The Quiet Man* and *The Sun Shines Bright*. Richard Hageman wrote the scores for *Stagecoach*, *The Long Voyage Home*, *The Fugitive*, *Fort Apache*, *3 Godfathers*, *She Wore a Yellow Ribbon* and *Wagon Master*.

64 The full lyrics are:

> The years creep slowly by, Lorena,
> The snow is on the grass again;
> The sun's low down the sky, Lorena,
> The frost gleams where the flow'rs have been.

But my heart throbs as warmly now
As when the summer days were nigh;
Oh! The sun can never dip so low,
A-down affection's cloudless sky.

A hundred months have passed, Lorena,
Since last I held that hand in mine,
And felt the pulse beat fast, Lorena,
Though mine beat faster far than thine.
A hundred months, 'twas flowery May
When up the hilly slope we climbed,
To watch the dying of the day,
And hear the distant church bell chime.

We loved each other then, Lorena,
More than we ever dared to tell;
And what we might have been, Lorena,
Had but our lovings prospered well –
But then, 'tis past, the years are gone,
I'll not call up their shadowy forms;
I'll say to them, 'lost years sleep on!
Sleep on! Nor heed life's pelting storms.'

Yes, these were words of love, Lorena,
They burn within my memory yet;
They touched some tender chords, Lorena,
Which thrill and tremble with regret.
'Twas not thy woman's heart that spoke;
Thy heart was always true to me;
A *duty*, stern and pressing, broke
The tie which linked my soul with thee.

The story of that past, Lorena,
Alas! I care not to repeat,
The hopes that could not last, Lorena,
They lived, but only lived to cheat.
I would not cause e'en one regret
To rankle in your bosom now;
For 'if we *try* we may forget'
Were words of thine long years ago.

It matters little now, Lorena,
The past is in th'eternal past,
Our heads will soon lie low, Lorena,
Life's tide is ebbing out so fast.
There is a future! O, thank God!
Of life this is so small a part!
'Tis dust to dust beneath the sod;
But there, *up there*, 'tis heart to heart.

65 See Jack Smith's sleeve notes for the CD of music from *The Searchers*, produced by the Film Music Archives, Brigham Young University (Warner Music FMA/MS101).
66 Ibid.
67 *The Last Hunt*, made the same year as *The Searchers*, has a score by Daniele Amfitheatrof which also uses 'Lorena' as its theme tune; at one point part of a verse is sung by an old-timer who plays the accordion:

> Oh! The sun can never dip so low,
> A-down affection's cloudless sky.

68 *The Searchers* offers a rich variety of hats. Apart from his straw hat down on the border, Ethan only once varies the black hat he wears at the beginning, changing to a brown one when he and Marty go to the Comanche camp and first meet Look. Mose, however, gets a different hat for each occasion; at first a nondescript brown one with a feather in it, then an old cavalry cap in the cantina, and finally a stovepipe hat, much too big for him, on the porch of the Jorgensens'. Charlie changes from an average cowboy hat to an impressively large stetson when he comes courting, and a brown derby for his wedding. Indians too wear hats. Twice we see Scar don his war bonnet, Look is given a brown homberg and her father gets a black stovepipe hat with a feather on it as part-exchange. The white women, on the other hand, only wear hats at the funeral.
69 This is presumably a Stetson, so named for its originator, John B. Stetson.
70 26 January 1955.
71 Edward Buscombe and Roberta Pearson (eds), *Back in the Saddle Again: New Essays on the Western* (London: BFI Publishing, 1998), p. 6.
72 See Gaberscek, *Il West di John Ford*, p. 85.
73 In a memo (26 January 1955) Ford had advised against ethnographic accuracy in the Indian costumes:

> It is important that the costumes of the Comanches be not exactly authentic. The Comanches were Plains Indians. ... They wore headdresses and eagle feathers ...

Colored blankets and shirts. I suggest for
their moccasins that they adopt the Navajo
knee, or three-quarter length boot … I
think Beetson [in charge of men's
wardrobe] should start looking through
Western Costume for leggings and war
bonnets. This has always been the bugaboo
of theWestern-Indian picture. Western
costume tries to fob off war bonnets made
of turkey feathers …
[So some degree of accuracy was required
after all.]

74 In a slightly macabre twist of fate, she and
Jeffrey Hunter would both suffer accidental
deaths at the age of forty-three, Hunter as the
result of a fall, Wood drowning at sea in an
incident that has never been satisfactorily
explained. Her sister Lana, who plays the
younger Debbie, later appeared in *Peyton Place*
on television, posed in *Playboy* with feathers in
her hair and starred in *Grayeagle* (1977), a kind
of low-budget version of *The Searchers*.
75 Mick Gidley, *Edward S. Curtis and the
North American Indian, Incorporated*
(Cambridge: Cambridge University Press,
1998), pp. 237–8.
76 Ford's memo of 27 January 1955 calls for 'a
real barndance stomp … not a professional
dance … but a real honest lusty dance'.
77 Stuart Byron quotes John Goldrosen in
Buddy Holly: His Life and Music as source for
the story that Holly's song 'That'll Be the Day'
was specifically based on Ethan's catch-phrase.
See Stuart Byron, '"The Searchers": Cult
Movie of the New Hollywood', *New York
Magazine*, 5 March 1979. See also Jack Smith's
CD sleeve notes, pp. 9–10. Only the first use of
the phrase appears in the script.
78 Jean-Luc Godard famously remarked:
'Mystery and fascination of this American
cinema … How can I hate John Wayne
upholding Goldwater and yet love him tenderly
when abruptly he takes Natalie Wood into his
arms in the last reel of *The Searchers*?'
Translated in Joseph McBride and Michael
Wilmington, *John Ford* (London: Secker &
Warburg, 1974), p. 148; originally in *Cahiers du
cinéma*, no. 184, November 1966.

79 Shurlock (Production Code Office, 1955).
Interestingly, Ford had at first wanted to cut
this scene, writing in a memo to Merian
Cooper (7 December 1955) 'I suggest it a
good idea to cut right after Duke says
"Let's go home, Debbie." Eliminate the
business with Ward and go right back to the
homecoming.'
80 *Hollywood: 'Out West'*, Thames Television,
4 March 1980.
81 Wills, *John Wayne*, pp. 259–60. Both Wills
and Gallagher misunderstand Wayne's gesture.
It's not, as they seem to think, the act of
walking away that is the homage to Harry
Carey, but, as Wayne makes clear to Brownlow,
the movement of the arm. Walking away is
nothing to do with Wayne's homage; it's to do
with the meaning of the film.
82 Wayne's gesture with his arm is not in the
script, nor is his walking away; indeed, the
scripted ending is entirely conventional:

> Ethan has Debbie on the pommel of his
> saddle, his arm supporting her, and she is
> asleep. Martin is riding beside them. Laurie
> comes running up to stare at Ethan and at
> the girl. He smiles and puts his finger to his
> lips – cautioning her against waking
> Debbie – and then he rides by. Laurie looks
> then at Martin. He doesn't know whether to
> smile or not; he just waits. And then she is
> beside him and she steps onto his stirruped
> foot and vaults up beside him and she kisses
> him just as she had on the day he left the
> graves to take up the search. And still
> holding her beside him, he rides slowly
> after Ethan and Debbie towards the house.
> FADE OUT.

83 All these reviews appeared on 31 May
1956.
84 All quotations from British reviews are
from *The Searchers* pressbook.
85 31 March 1956.
86 17 March 1956.
87 13 March 1956.
88 13 March 1956.
89 Ford papers, Lilly Library, Box 6, file 22.
90 Joel Finler and David Pirie, *Anatomy of the
Movies* (New York: Macmillan, 1981).

91 Lindsay Anderson, '*The Searchers*', *Sight and Sound*, 26/2, Autumn, 1956; Anderson, *About John Ford*, p. 152.

92 Pauline Kael, *5001 Nights at the Movies: A Guide from A to Z* (New York: Holt, Rinehart & Winston, 1982), p. 517.

93 David Thomson, 'Open and Shut: A Fresh Look at *The Searchers*', *Film Comment*, 33/4, July/August 1997; David Thomson, *A Biographical Dictionary of Film* (London: André Deutsch, 1994), pp. 256–8.

94 Coming in behind *Citizen Kane*, *La Règle du jeu*, *Tokyo Story* and *Vertigo*.

95 Byron, '"The Searchers".

96 Nor are films the only examples of inter-textuality. In addition to Buddy Holly's song, already mentioned, in the immediate wake of the film's release Dell Comics produced a full-colour comic book version of the film (with some significant changes; Ethan doesn't try to kill Debbie at the stream, nor does he scalp Scar, and at the end he is not excluded). Jonathan Lethem's recent novel *Girl in Landscape* (1998), set on the frontier of an imaginary planet in the future, features a central character named Efram Nugent, with recognisably Ethan-type characteristics.

97 Bogdanovich, *John Ford*, pp. 94–5.

98 In 1969, in a much-discussed article, the French journal *Cahiers du Cinéma* proposed a category of film in which

> an internal criticism is taking place ... if one looks beyond its apparent formal coherence, one can see that it is riddled with cracks: it is splitting under an internal tension which is simply not there in an ideologically innocuous film. ... if [the film-maker] sees his film simply as a blow in favour of liberalism, it will be recuperated instantly by the ideology; if, on the other hand, he conceives and realizes it on the deeper level of imagery, there is a chance that it will turn out to be more disruptive.

Ford was given as an example of a director who makes this type of film, and *The Searchers* would seem to be a prime candidate for this category. See Nick Browne (ed.), *Cahiers du Cinéma Vol. 3, 1969–1972: The Politics of Representation* (London: Routledge/BFI, 1990), p. 63.

CREDITS

. . . .

The Searchers

USA
1956
US Release
26 May 1956
Distributor
Warner Bros. Pictures Inc
British Release
23 September 1956

©C.V.Whitney Pictures Inc
Production Companies
Warner Bros. Pictures
presents
The C.V.Whitney Picture
Executive Producer
Merian C. Cooper
Associate Producer
Patrick Ford
Production Supervisor
Lowell J. Farrell
Location Scout
Robert Lee 'Lefty' Hough
Director
John Ford
Assistant Directors
Wingate Smith
2nd Unit, Gunnison,
Colorado:
Edward O'Fearna
Script Supervisor
Robert Gary
Screenplay
Frank S. Nugent
Based on the story
'The Avenging Texans' and
the novel by Alan LeMay
Director of Photography
Winton C. Hoch
**2nd Unit Director of
Photography**
Alfred Gilks
**Technicolor Colour
Consultant**
James Gooch

Camera Operators
Al Greene
2nd Unit, Gunnison,
Colorado:
Arch R. Dalzell,
Buddy Weiler
Camera Technicians
2nd Unit, Gunnison,
Colorado:
Gene Polito, George Dye
Assistant Camera
2nd Unit, Gunnison,
Colorado:
Elmer Faubian
Camera Mechanic
2nd Unit, Gunnison,
Colorado:
Frank Shriner
Head Grip
2nd Unit, Gunnison,
Colorado:
Carl Gibson
Assistant Grips
2nd Unit, Gunnison,
Colorado:
Jack Chambers,
Pete Barnard, Larry Hughes
Battery Man
2nd Unit, Gunnison,
Colorado:
John Funk
Stills Photography
Alexander Kahle
Special Effects
George Brown
2nd Unit, Gunnison,
Colorado:
Dave Koehler
Film Editor
Jack Murray
Art Directors
Frank Hotaling,
James Basevi
Set Decorator
Victor Gangelin
Properties
Dudley Holmes

Props
Art Cole
Assistant Props
2nd Unit, Gunnison,
Colorado:
Jack Owens
Labourer
2nd Unit, Gunnison,
Colorado:
Bob Woods
Men's Wardrobe
Frank Beetson
Women's Wardrobe
Ann Peck
Wardrobe Assistant
2nd Unit, Gunnison,
Colorado:
Charles Arrico
Make-up
Web Overlander
2nd Unit, Gunnison,
Colorado:
Burris Grimwood
Make-up Assistants
Jack Obringer
2nd Unit, Gunnison,
Colorado:
Joe Hadley
Hairdresser
Fae Smith
Music
Max Steiner
Orchestrations
Murray Cutter
Soundtrack
'The Searchers' by Stan
Jones, sung by The Sons of
the Pioneers; 'Skip to My
Lou' (trad.), 'Shall We
Gather at the River' (trad.)
Sound
Hugh McDowell,
Howard Wilson
First Aid
2nd Unit, Gunnison,
Colorado:
Nathan Stufflebeam

Radio Man
2nd Unit, Gunnison,
Colorado:
W.C. Stokes
Stunts
William J. Cartledge,
Chuck Hayward,
Slim Hightower,
Fred Kennedy,
Frank McGrath,
Dale Van Sickle,
Henry Wills, Terry Wilson
Stand-ins
Ray Cordell, Betty Danko,
Grace Ritchie,
Harry Tenbrook
Wranglers
Glen Holly, Robert Reeves,
Desmond Lane,
Logan Morris,
Ellsworth Vierelle

Cast
John Wayne
Ethan Edwards
Jeffrey Hunter
Martin Pawley
Vera Miles
Laurie Jorgensen
Ward Bond
Captain the Reverend
Samuel Johnson Clayton
Natalie Wood
Debbie Edwards

John Qualen
Lars Jorgensen
Olive Carey
Mrs Jorgensen
Henry Brandon
Chief Scar/Cicatriz
Ken Curtis
Charlie McCorry
Harry Carey Jr
Brad Jorgensen
Antonio Moreno
Emilio Gabriel Fernandez y
Figueroa
Hank Worden
Mose Harper
Beulah Archuletta
Look/Wild Goose Flying in
the Night Sky
Walter Coy
Aaron Edwards
Dorothy Jordan
Martha Edwards
Pippa Scott
Lucy Edwards
Patrick Wayne
Lieutenant Greenhill
Lana Wood
Debbie as a child

[uncredited]
Jack Pennick
private
Peter Mamakos
Jerem Futterman
William Steele
Nesby
Cliff Lyons
Colonel Greenhill
Chuck Roberson
Ranger Lawrence
Ruth Clifford
deranged woman
Mae Marsh
woman at fort
Nacho Galindo
Mexican bartender
Carmen D'Antonio
dancer in cantina

Robert Lyden
Ben Edwards
Frank McGrath
soldier
Terry Wilson
ranger
Away Luna
Billy Yellow
Bob Many Mules
Exactly Sonnie Betsuie
Feather Hat Jr
Harry Black Horse
Jack Tin Horn
Many Mules Son
Percy Shooting Star
Pete Gray Eyes
Pipe Line Begishe
Smile White Sheep
Comanche
Joe Rickson
Bud Cokes
William Forrest
extras
Peter Ortiz
General Custer – role
deleted

10,681 feet
119 minutes

Colour by
Technicolor
VistaVision

BIBLIOGRAPHY

. . . .

This is not a complete listing, only of the works I have found most useful.

Anderson, Lindsay. '*The Searchers*', *Sight and Sound*, 26/2, Autumn, 1956.

Anderson, Lindsay. *About John Ford* (London: Plexus, 1981).

Bogdanovich, Peter. *John Ford* (London: Studio Vista, 1967).

Byron, Stuart. '"The Searchers": Cult Movie of the New Hollywood', *New York Magazine*, 5 March 1979.

Card, James Van Dyck. '*The Searchers* by Alan LeMay and by John Ford', *Literature/Film Quarterly*, 16, 1988.

Carey Jr, Harry. *Company of Heroes: My Life as an Actor in the John Ford Stock Company* (Lanham, Maryland: Madison Books, 1996).

Clauss, James J. 'Descent into Hell: Mythic Paradigms in *The Searchers*', unpublished essay.

Eckstein, Arthur M. 'Incest and Miscegenation in *The Searchers* (1956) and *The Unforgiven* (1959)', unpublished.

Eckstein, Arthur M. 'John Ford's *The Searchers* (1956) from Novel to Screenplay to Screen', *Cinema Journal*, 38/1, Fall 1998.

Ford, Dan. *Pappy: The Life of John Ford* (New York: Da Capo, 1998).

Gaberscek, Carlo. *Il West di John Ford* (Udine: Arti Grafiche Friulane, 1994).

Gallagher, Tag. *John Ford: The Man and His Films* (Berkeley: University of California Press, 1986).

Henderson, Brian. '*The Searchers*: An American Dilemma', *Film Quarterly*, 34/2, Winter 1980–1.

Hutson, Richard. 'Sermons in Stone: Monument Valley in *The Searchers*' in Leonard Engel (ed.), *The Big Empty: Essays on Western Landscapes as Narrative* (Albuquerque: University of New Mexico Press, 1994).

Lehman, Peter. 'Texas 1868/America 1956: *The Searchers*' in Peter Lehman (ed.), *Close Viewings* (Tallahassee: Florida State University Press, 1990).

Lehman, Peter. '"There's no way of knowing" – Analysis of *The Searchers*' in William Luhr and Peter Lehman, *Authorship and Narrative in the Cinema* (New York: G.P.Putnam's Sons, 1977).

LeMay, Alan. *The Searchers* (London: Corgi, 1963).

Leutrat, Jean-Louis. *John Ford: La Prisonnière du désert, une tapisserie navajo* (Paris: Adam Biro, 1990).

Maltby, Richard. 'John Ford and the Indians; or, Tom Doniphon's History Lesson' in Mick Gidley (ed.), *Representing Others: White Views of Indigenous Peoples* (Exeter: University of Exeter Press, 1992).

Maltby, Richard and Craven, Ian. *Hollywood Cinema: An Introduction* (Oxford: Blackwell, 1995).

McBride, Joseph and Wilmington, Michael. *John Ford* (London: Secker & Warburg, 1974).

Pye, Douglas. 'Double Vision: Miscegenation and Point of View in *The Searchers*' in Ian Cameron and Douglas Pye (eds), *The Movie Book of the Western* (London: Studio Vista, 1996).

Reed, Allen C. 'John Ford Makes Another Movie Classic in Monument Valley', *Arizona Highways*, April 1956.

Roth, M. '"Yes, My Darling Daughter": Gender, Miscegenation and Generation in John Ford's *The Searchers*', *New Orleans Review*, 18, 1991.

Sarris, Andrew. '*The Searchers*', *Film Comment*, 7/1, Spring 1971.

Skerry, P. J. 'What Makes a Man to Wander? Ethan Edwards of John Ford's *The Searchers*', *New Orleans Review*, 18, 1991.

Stern, Lesley. *The Scorsese Connection* (London: BFI Publishing, 1995), chapter 3: 'A Glitter of Putrescence'.

Thomson, David. 'Open and Shut: A Fresh Look at *The Searchers*', *Film Comment*, 33/4, July/August 1997.

Tompkins, Jane. *West of Everything: The Inner Life of Westerns* (New York: Oxford University Press, 1992).

Wills, Garry. *John Wayne: The Politics of Celebrity* (London: Faber and Faber, 1997), chapter 20: 'The Fury of Ethan'.

Winkler, Martin M. 'Tragic Features in John Ford's *The Searchers*', *Classics and Cinema*, 35/1, 1991.

ALSO PUBLISHED

If you would like further information about future BFI Film Classics or about other books on film, media and popular culture from BFI Publishing, please write to:

BFI Film Classics
BFI Publishing
21 Stephen Street
London W1P 2LN

BFI Film Classics '...could scarcely be improved upon ... informative, intelligent, jargon-free companions.'
The Observer

Each book in the BFI Publishing Film Classics series honours a great film from the history of world cinema. With new titles published each year, the series is rapidly building into a collection representing some of the best writing on film. If you would like to receive further information about future Film Classics or about other books on film, media and popular culture from BFI Publishing, please fill in your name and address and return this card to the BFI.* (No stamp required if posted in the UK, Channel Islands, or Isle of Man.)

NAME

ADDRESS

POSTCODE

WHICH *BFI FILM CLASSIC* DID YOU BUY?

* In North America, please return your card to: Indiana University Press, Attn: LPB, 601 N. Morton Street, Bloomington, IN 47401-3797

Montage (slo-mo/ real time,
Scenes of mayhem
battle, galloping horses, nightmare
to Neil Diamond's waking
"Solitary Man"

extreme Leone
"eyes" close-ups.

BFI Publishing
21 Stephen Street
FREEPOST 7
LONDON
W1E 4AN